PLAYSONG

Bible Time

for Fours

"Let's Grow With God"

Spring Quarter:
I Grow to Know Jesus

by

Karyn Henley

PLAYSONGS™ Bible Time for Fours: Let's Grow with God

© 2003, 2010 Karyn Henley. All rights reserved. Exclusively administered by Child Sensitive Communication, LLC. PO Box 150806, Nashville, TN 37215-0806

Written and illustrated by Karyn Henley

Layout by Kristi J. West.

PLAYSONGS and dandelion logo are trademarks of Karyn Henley.

ALL RIGHTS RESERVED. No part of this publication may be reproduced, stored in a retrieval system, or transmitted in any form or by any means (electronic, mechanical, photocopying, recording or otherwise) without prior written permission from the publisher.

A word about photocopying:

Permission is granted to photocopy patterns and hand-out pages for classroom use.

Otherwise, the purchaser <u>DOES NOT</u> have the right to photocopy, reprint, give away, sell or share this publication or the content herein. If you obtained this publication from anywhere other than **karynhenley.com,** or a Karyn Henley Resources exhibit booth, you have a pirated copy.

Please help stop copyright infringement by reporting suspected pirating of this publication to: **office@karynhenley.com**.

We try to provide high-quality lesson plans at an affordable price for ministry purposes. God has provided us the protection of U.S. Copyright law, and has ordained that "those who work deserve to be fed." (Matthew 10:10). **Please do not deprive us of our livelihood by making unauthorized copies from this manual.** A photocopy license is available for a reasonable fee. Please contact Karyn Henley Resources for details.

For more information about this curriculum, contact:

Karyn Henley Resources
PO Box 150806
Nashville, TN 37215-0806
1-888-573-3953 (toll-free U.S.)
www.KarynHenley.com

I GROW TO KNOW JESUS

Scripture for Spring Quarter: "Grow knowing Jesus." 2 Peter 3:18, ICB (simplified)

Introduction: Let's Look at Some Basics	i
Walk Through a Lesson	ii
Adapting for Daily Classroom Setting	v
Connect with Parents	vi

Lessons:

1.	Jesus Grew	1
2.	Jesus Does Amazing Things Called Miracles – Water Changes into Wine	7
3.	Jesus is a Good Friend – Jesus Eats at Matthew's House	12
4.	Jesus is a Teacher – Sermon on the Mount	17
5.	Jesus is Like a Good Shepherd – Good Shepherd, Lost Sheep, Psalm 23	24
6.	*Palm Sunday: Jesus is Our King – Triumphal Entry	30
7.	*Easter: Jesus is Our Savior – Jesus' Death & Resurrection	37
8.	Jesus is a Healer – Jesus Heals a Man's Hand	43
9.	Jesus is Worthy of Praise – Jesus Heals a Bent-Over Woman	48
10.	Jesus Cares About Us – Jesus Walks on Water	54
11.	Jesus Loves All People – The Woman at the Well	59
12.	We Love and Worship Jesus – Mary Anoints Jesus with Perfume	65
13.	Jesus Will Come Back Someday – The Ascension	70

About Materials	78
A Week-by-Week List of Materials You Will Need	78

* These two lessons may be moved to the appropriate week for the current calendar year.

INTRODUCTION

Welcome to **PlaySongs Bible Time for Four Year Olds**. The theme of this four-quarter curriculum is "Let's Grow With God":

        Quarter 1 - I Grow
        Quarter 2 - I Discover God's World As I Grow
        Quarter 3 - I Grow to Know Jesus
        Quarter 4 - I Grow Up Helping

Let's Look at Some Basics:

- **Fours don't understand the flow of time.**

    For a four year old, the time from one Sunday to the next is a long time. Preschoolers don't string together, in time order, the Bible stories told from week to week. When you say, "A long time ago, there was a man named Abraham," the preschool mind interprets it as yesterday. To them, yesterday was a long time ago. So Bible stories are not covered in biblical order in this curriculum. Instead, PlaySongs Bible Time for Fours incorporates simple Bible stories which support the weekly age-appropriate themes. The four year old, for the first time, realizes that he is growing and will not always be little. Fours will often come to class every week and announce their age. So themes focus on growing: growing up knowing God is with me, growing up praying, growing up helping, and so on.

- **Fours interact more cooperatively with classmates.**

    Unlike three year olds (who play side by side with others, yet not really together), four year olds are usually ready to play with a friend or classmate. They are learning how to cooperate. They are better able to control themselves than they were at three. However, fours are still quite focused on their own wishes, and they are usually very active and assertive in pursuing their interests. This curriculum takes advantage of these changes, encouraging children to include God in their everyday exploits, helping them learn that God is in control of life and that even growing children can choose to honor Him.

- **Fours learn by action and repetition.**

    Fours are active and learn by hearing, seeing, smelling, tasting, touching and doing. As with younger preschoolers, if fours hear words, rhymes, and songs repeated over and over again, they will repeat these words, rhymes, and songs themselves. So **PlaySongs Bible Time** for Fours relies heavily on learning through a variety of sensory activities and repetition. Teachers model and repeat the important themes of the lessons and guide the children into experiences that enrich their understanding of how to grow up knowing God.

- **Fours are sensitive to music: melody and rhythm.**

    PlaySongs Bible Time is a song-filled curriculum, just as the name implies. A preschooler's short attention span can often be held and strengthened by songs when the child seems oblivious to spoken words. The simple melodies and rhythms repeated in childhood stay in the heart and mind for a lifetime. So key truths, themes, and verses in **PlaySongs Bible Time** are presented not only in spoken words, but also in song.

- **Fours are attracted to sensory experiences and action.**
    The attention span of a four year old may be noticeably longer than it was at three. But fours are exuberant and often have trouble sitting still and focusing on an activity. They are more likely to stick with an activity or story if it's interesting, active, musical, colorful, tasty, and fun. Occasionally children need someone to draw their attention to these activities. Teachers may find that when they themselves engage in the desired activity and have fun doing it, the children will be drawn in naturally. **PlaySongs Bible Time** has many activity choices which can expand and contract to fit children's needs.

- **Fours need supervision and (sometimes) help.**
    Fours enjoy doing as much as possible for themselves. However, they still need help and/or supervision as they learn. A teacher-child ratio of **one teacher for every six to eight four-year-olds** is very important for quality care-giving. When recruiting helpers and teachers, remember that grandparents and teenagers are often overlooked, but can be valuable members of a teaching team.

WALK THROUGH A LESSON

Memory Verse for the Quarter
There is one Bible verse for each quarter, emphasizing the quarter's theme. The verse is sung to a simple melody. With repetition week after week, it becomes a memory verse that the children can sing themselves.

Scripture   Each story or theme also has a scripture that is relevant. These are also often set to music, but are more focused to the week's lesson that to the quarter theme.

Bible Story   The Bible stories are very simple, each concentrating on a single incident or truth that is relevant to fours. Still, teachers should read the scripture reference in preparation for classtime, asking God to renew their own awe at His simple truths.

Goal   The goals for fours are simple, focused on growing up knowing and following God and His Son Jesus.

Today's Teacher Task
This tells the teacher exactly the phrases that need to be repeated over and over again as appropriate during every activity throughout class time. These phrases point out and describe the focus of the lesson. The repetition of these phrases and the recommended songs will help the children learn the lesson for the day.

INTRODUCTION
Class time starts when the first child arrives. Teachers should be available and ready to greet each child and his or her parents as they arrive. One teacher can already be involved in the introductory activity as the children arrive, so that there is something of active sensory interest going on that will appeal to the child's desire to watch or participate. Encourage the children to join this activity.

© Karyn Henley. All rights reserved.

You may prefer to have two or three activities from the lesson already in progress so that the children can be guided into more than one group. Or you may allow the children to begin their class time in free play with some of the materials that will be part of the activities later in class (blocks or trucks, toy animals, etc.) In this case, as you supervise their play, say the phrases from the Teacher Task for the day when appropriate. This is one of the most important things you'll do related to the goal of the lesson, and it can be repeated at any time during class, including this introduction time.

LARGE GROUP TIME

Use the song "Come to the Circle" as the cue for the children to gather. If they have gone through the PlaySongs Bible Time curriculum for threes, they will already be familiar with the song and will know that it calls them to gather as a group. If you have small, comfortable chairs, they can sit in these for the group time. Or you can let them sit around you on a rug. It will be helpful to gather for the large group time in the same area of the room each week so the children will know what to expect. You may find it helpful to provide a carpet square on the floor for each child to sit on in order to help each child find a place quickly and sit in an organized way. You can often find these from discarded carpet samples at a carpet store.

BIBLE STORY

Simple, interesting and meaningful. These are principles to keep in mind when telling Bible stories to young children. Be expressive. Tell the story with a sense of wonder and awe and an eagerness to share with the children. Show pictures and objects. Let children touch and hold and be involved as much as possible.

Songs and Movement

You will find the same songs recommended in almost every lesson. Children feel comfortable with routine and enjoy knowing what to expect. As you sing these songs week after week, the children will come to know them and will be inclined to join as you sing. Feel free to substitute other songs that you know are appropriate for young children. Songs with hand motions are especially interesting for them.

Prayer

Model prayer by folding your hands and bowing your head. Ask for a volunteer to say the prayer, or ask the children to say the prayer after you, phrase by phrase.

EXPLORE-A-BINS

Although you may have different areas of your room specifically dedicated to block play, housekeeping play, or books, each week concentrates on specific props that can be used in these areas as well as in other activities. Bins can help you bring new activity tools and props into the room, and they provide a way to catch attention as you start a new activity:

"Let's see what's in our art bin today."
"I wonder what's in here. Jonathan, can you look and see?"
"Open this bin, Clay, and let's find out what's inside."

You don't have to use all the suggested activities each week. Choose the ones you want based on the materials you have available, the help you have available, and the interests of the children.

Use large plastic tub-like bins with snap-on lids. They don't all have to be the same size, although for easy storage, it will help if they are stackable. Recommended bins are:

The Art Bin - The art activities are varied, and many are sensory in nature. Children will be able to take their artwork home to show what they've done and tell about the lesson. For some activities, smocks are recommended. These can be made out of old shirts. A plastic tablecloth makes a good work surface.

The Science-Math Bin - This bin contains items that challenge the child's curiosity in the area of counting, nature, building, matching, and other skills that are foundational to learning in science and math.

The Look and Listen Bin - This bin contains books, CDs, and DVDs that encourage the child to look and listen. This is a quieter, less active time.

The Creative Movement Bin - These songs and rhymes are participatory. Sometimes CD's/DVDs are recommended, but they are used to encourage the children to move actively in response to what they see and hear. Many of the songs and rhymes require no materials.

The Game Bin - This bin contains items that encourage the child to participate in cooperation with other children as you lead them in one or more games. Sometimes there are no materials required for this activity.

The Snack Bin - The recommended snack for each week provides another opportunity to emphasize the theme of the lesson.

If you have a large number of children:
Place the explore-a-bins in different areas of the room. Assign one teacher to six to eight children. Teachers move their group through the different areas, doing the activities with their children, or teachers help their own group as the entire class of children does the same activity.

If you have only a few children:
Bring out the explore-a-bins one by one, doing the activities together. You may still choose to move to different locations in the room for different bins, just to provide a change of setting.

All activities relate to God's ways and how we can choose to follow God's ways.

Materials:
Most of the materials recommended are simple, easy to find, and inexpensive. A complete list of materials for this quarter can be found in the appendix.

Procedure:
As you do the activities with the children, remember to relax and have fun. To them, this is directed play.

Discuss:
Four year olds are usually quite willing to "discuss" with you. Some of the recommended

questions are close-ended for the purpose of review. However, many discussion questions are also open-ended. They require more than just a "yes" or "no" answer and encourage discussion. Be open to children wondering and supposing and giving answers that you may not have thought about. Also be ready for children to ask you questions. The most important thing to remember at this time is the Teacher Task for the day. Try to bring the discussion back around to a place at which you can repeat the phrase for the day. Also try to use recommended songs to support your point.

> Note: A CD is available for the some of the songs and action rhymes included in this book. When a song or action rhyme is available on the companion Song Reference CD, a note will be included as well as the track number for the song or action rhyme. For example:
>
> Sing "Come to the Circle" (page 6/Track #9)
>
> The Playsongs® Bible Time Song Reference CD for Toddler/Twos is available for purchase by calling toll free 1-888-573-3953 or by ordering at www.KarynHenley.com.

>
>
> TIMESAVER =
>
> Remember that you don't have to do every activity listed. Several activities are recommended so that you can choose which ones are suitable for your needs. **T** beside an activity indicates that it is a **Timesaver**, taking less time for preparation. In some of the activities, there is a **Timesaver** option. In others, the original activity is a **Timesaver**, and the option gives you opportunity to expand the activity.

Adapting PLAYSONGS™ Bible Time Curriculum for a Daily Classroom Setting

The PLAYSONGS Bible Time Curriculum is easily adaptable for use in the daily classroom setting. Each age level provides 52 weeks of lessons! Simply follow the sample lesson plan below for a five-day format.

<u>Theme of the Week</u>: Title of Lesson

<u>Scripture to Memorize</u>: Located at the beginning of each week's lesson plan

<u>Introductory Activity</u>: Incorporate this activity into one of the daily Large Group Times

<u>Large Group Time</u>: This includes the Bible Story, Songs and Movement time, and a Prayer time

<u>Explore-A-Bin Activities</u>: Choose one or two activities from the assortment of activities included in each week's lesson. If you prefer a more structured routine, choose the activities in the same order

each day of the week. For example, Tuesday is science-math activity day. Wednesday is arts and crafts day, and so on. Choose as many activities as classtime allows. If all Explore-A-Bin™ activities have been completed by mid-week, the children can repeat the ones they especially enjoyed or supplement with activities from Karyn Henley's Bible story activity books.

Sample Week

These are only suggestions. Do these activities in any order you prefer or incorporate your own ideas.

Day 1   Have Large Group Time followed by the Introduction activity and one Explore-A-Bin activity.

Day 2   During Large Group Time repeat the Bible story but let the children fill in the "blanks" as you tell it. Choose one or two Explore-A-Bin activities.

Day 3   During Large Group Time have the children act out the week's Bible story. Choose one or two Explore-A-Bin activities.

Day 4   During Large Group Time allow the children to take turns telling the week's Bible story. Choose one or two Explore-A-Bin activities.

Day 5   For Large Group Time choose a book, CD, or DVD from the "Look and Listen Bin" to read or listen to. Discuss how the book, CD, or DVD relates to the Bible story. If time allows choose another Explore-A-Bin activity.

CONNECT WITH PARENTS

Parents enjoy knowing what their children are doing and learning. Many parents feel more confident leaving their children with you if they know what will be happening in your class. You can enrich the children's family life by communicating with the parents. There are several ways to do this.

- **Tote Notes**
Keep pens and a stack of large colored index cards close by, but out of the children's reach. When a child says or does something new or fun or interesting, jot it down on a note and hand it to the parents as they pick the child up, or mail it during the week. If you can't do this during class, try to remember after class, and prepare the note for next week.

- **Look At Me! Board**
Keep a camera loaded and handy to take photos of children doing interesting things in class. Or have a volunteer come into class periodically to take photos. Then post them on a bulletin board outside the classroom so parents can see their children in class.

- **Parent Observers**
Invite parents to come and observe your class in progress. Many parents enjoy it so much that they volunteer to become helpers and teachers.

Lesson 1

Jesus Grew

Memory Verse for the Quarter: "Grow knowing Jesus." 2 Peter 3:18, ICB, simplified

Scripture "(Jesus) grew taller. People liked him, and he pleased God."
Luke 2:52, ICB

Bible Story Jesus grows, Luke 2:52, Matthew 13:55, 56

Goal Learn that Jesus was once a little boy, and He grew up like we do.

Today's Teacher Task
- Point out things that indicate growth.
- Repeat as often as appropriate:

  Jesus was once a little boy. (hands to side)
  He grew up like we do. (stretch up high)

INTRODUCTION

Materials: a board about 1' wide by 3' long, two bricks or sturdy blocks the same size, a roll of heavy-duty paper towels, tape or reusable adhesive (Plasti-tak or Tac 'n stik), postable sticky notes, a pen

Do: Place one brick under each end of the board to make a balance beam. Help the children walk across the board and jump off the end. Roll out the paper towels until they are taller than the tallest child. Tear off this length and hang it on wall or door until the bottom just touches the ground. Ask each child in turn to stand with his or her back to the paper towels. Mark the child's height, then place a sticky note there with the child's name on it.

Discuss: Talk about growing taller and older. Ask the children when their birthdays are. Ask if they have brothers and/or sisters and whether their brothers/sisters are taller or shorter than they are.

LARGE GROUP TIME

Sing "Come to the Circle" (page 6/track #9), and gather the children together in a large group.

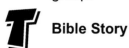 **Bible Story**

Materials: a Bible with a bookmark at Matthew 13:55

© Karyn Henley. All rights reserved.

Do: In class, open the Bible to Matthew 13:55 and say: **Here's where the Bible tells about Jesus. Where was baby Jesus born? Did He stay a baby? Jesus grew to be a boy. He was a boy in a family.** Read what the people said about Jesus in Matthew 13:53–56. **Jesus had brothers and sisters.** Ask the children to raise their hands if they have brothers and sisters. **Jesus' daddy was a carpenter. He built things. What job does your dad and/or mom do? Jesus was once a little boy. He grew up like we do.**

Songs and Movement

Sing the memory verse song, "Growing Knowing Jesus" (page 6/track #28).

Now ask the children to follow you as you sing the following song to the tune of "Here We Go 'Round the Mulberry Bush" (track #86).

This is the way that Jesus grew, **Jesus grew,** **Jesus grew,** **This is the way that Jesus grew,** **And I am growing, too.**	(squat and slowly rise)
This is the way that Jesus walked. . . **And I am walking, too.**	(walk around the room)
This is the way that Jesus prayed. . . **And I am praying, too.**	(fold hands and bow head)

Now say, **The Bible tells us, "Jesus obeyed everything his parents told him"** (Luke 2:51). Continue singing:

Jesus did what Mommy said **What Mommy said,** **What Mommy said,** **Jesus did what Mommy said,** **And that's what I do too.**	(walk back around room)
Jesus did what Daddy said. . . **And that's what I do too.**	(walk back around room and sit)

Prayer

Ask the children to fold their hands and pray the words after you:
   Dear God, Thank you that Jesus grew up. Amen.

EXPLORE-A-BINS
Choose from these activities. Use them in the order that best suits your needs.

1. The Art Bin: Knuckle Print

Materials: paper, preschool washable liquid paint, paper plates, paper towels and hand wipes

Do: Give each child a piece of paper. Pour paint onto paper plates (one color of paint per plate) so that the paint barely covers the bottom of the plate. Ask the children to look at the backs of their hands. Point out their knuckles. Ask them to count their knuckles and then make fists. Show the children how to press their knuckles into the paint and then onto the paper to make designs.

Discuss: Ask, **When you grow, do your knuckles grow too?** (Hold your own hand in a fist so they can compare the size of their knuckles to the size of yours.) **How can you tell you are growing? Who made your body so it will grow? Was Jesus ever your size? What was Jesus' family like when he was a little boy? Jesus was once a little boy. He grew up like we do.** Sing "Growing Knowing Jesus" (page 6/track #28).

2. The Science-Math Bin: Bigger and Smaller

Materials: different sizes of shoes, socks, shirts, hats (some for babies, some for older children)

Do: Ask the children to arrange the shirts in order from small to large. Ask them to do the same with the shoes, socks, and hats. Or you can ask them to arrange them from large to small.

Discuss: Ask, **Are you growing bigger or smaller? How have you changed from the time you were a baby? What can you do now that you couldn't do when you were a baby? Who makes us grow? Was Jesus ever your size? What was Jesus' family like when he was a little boy? Jesus was once a little boy. He grew up like we do.** Sing "Growing Knowing Jesus" (page 6/track #28).

3. The Look and Listen Bin: Growing

Materials: books, CDs and/or DVDs about growing, CD/DVD player

You may choose your own books and CDs/DVDs. Some suggestions are:
   Here Are My Hands by Bill Martin, Jr. and John Archambault
   The Carrot Seed by Ruth Krauss
Is It Larger? Is It Smaller? by Tana Hoban
I Can Fly by Ruth Krauss
"Samuel's Growing," from My Thank You Bible Stories & Songs CD by Karyn Henley
"Grow, Grow, Grow" and "God Made Food," from PlaySongs: Grow, Grow, Grow, CD/DVD by Karyn Henley
"Special Chair," from PlaySongs: Tiny Treasures, CD/DVD by Karyn Henley
"Praise the Lord," from PlaySongs: I Feel Like a Giggle, CD/DVD by Karyn Henley

© Karyn Henley. All rights reserved.

Do: Read the book(s) to the children or let them look at the pictures, and ask them to describe the things in the book that grow. Listen to any CDs/DVDs you've chosen.

Discuss: Talk about growing and what children can do as they grow. Say, **Jesus was once a little boy. He grew up like we do.** Sing "Growing Knowing Jesus" (page 6/track #28).

4. The Creative Movement Bin: I'm Growing

Materials: a bright light, lamp, or slide projector, sheets to put over any windows to darken the room if necessary, option: CD and player

Do: Encourage the children to copy you as you do the following action songs.

I'm Growing   (to the tune of "It's Raining, It's Pouring"/track #39)

I'm growing, I'm growing,	(clap)
And God's love is showing.	
I once was small,	(squat)
But now I'm tall,	(pop up)
Just look at how I'm growing.	(stretch up high)

For more verses, sing the same words, but jump instead of clapping. Twirl on another verse, tiptoe on another.

Watch Me Grow!   (to the tune of "Are You Sleeping?"/track #90)

I am* growing, I am growing,	
Did you know? Did you know?	
Legs are getting longer,	(pat thighs)
Arms are getting stronger.	(make muscles with arms)
Watch me* grow! Watch me grow!	(stretch high)

*Substitute children's names for subsequent verses.

Now turn on the bright light, and turn off the room light. Don't let the children touch or stare into the bright light. Shine the light at the wall, and let the children stand between the light and the wall so their bodies make shadows. Ask them to move closer to the wall. Point out that their shadows get smaller. Ask them to move closer to the light. Point out that their shadows grow. Sing or play a CD so the children can dance and watch their shadows.

Discuss: Point out how the shadows grow. Tell the children that they can hop and jump and tiptoe, because they are growing bigger. Say, **Jesus was once a little boy. He grew up like we do.** Sing "Growing Knowing Jesus" (page 6/track #28).

© Karyn Henley. All rights reserved.

5. The Game Bin: Balloon Base

Materials: five different colors of balloons, tape, a measuring tape or yardstick, a jump rope

Do: While the children watch, inflate the balloons. Point out how small the balloons are at first and then how big they grow. Tape the balloons up at five different places in the room. Then give children directions to follow to get to the balloons. Tell them to hop to the red balloon. When they are there, ask them to crawl to the green balloon. Then tell them to fly to the yellow balloon, march to the purple balloon, tiptoe to the orange balloon.

Let children take turns jumping across the floor. Measure how far they can go in one jump. Then ask two helpers to hold a rope about six inches off the ground. Let children take turns jumping over it. When they have all jumped over, raise it an inch or two. Let them try jumping over again. Keep on until the rope is too high to jump. Then let them take turns going under it.

Discuss: Ask, **How does your body grow? What can you do now that you couldn't do when you were little? What will you be able to do when you grow up? Who helps you grow? Did Jesus grow? What was his family like when He was a little boy? Jesus was once a little boy. He grew up like we do.** Sing "Growing Knowing Jesus" (page 6/track #28).

6. The Snack Bin: Foods that Help Me Grow

Materials: mandarin orange segments, bananas, apple slices, cheese squares, juice, paper plates and cups, paper towels, hand wipes, knife for teacher to use

Do: Ask the children to clean their hands with wipes. Pray, thanking God for Jesus and for a good snack to help us grow. Serve the snack.

Discuss: Describe the foods and tell the children that these foods will help us grow big and strong. Ask, **How does your body grow? What can you do now that you couldn't do when you were little? What will you be able to do when you grow up? Who helps you grow? Did Jesus grow? What was his family like when He was a little boy? Jesus was once a little boy. He grew up like we do.** Sing "Growing Knowing Jesus" (page 6/track #28).

Come to the Circle (CD Track #9)

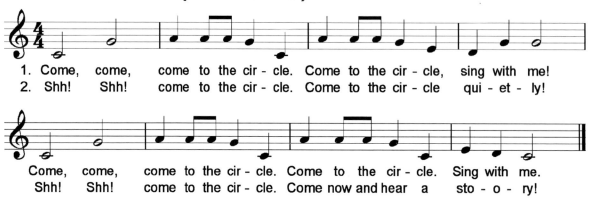

1. Come, come, come to the cir-cle. Come to the cir-cle, sing with me!
2. Shh! Shh! come to the cir-cle. Come to the cir-cle qui-et-ly!

Come, come, come to the cir-cle. Come to the cir-cle. Sing with me.
Shh! Shh! come to the cir-cle. Come now and hear a sto-o-ry!

Growing Knowing Jesus (CD Track #28)

1. I am grow-ing know-ing Je-sus. I am grow-ing ev-'ry day.
2. I am grow-ing know-ing Je-sus. I am grow-ing know-ing God.

I am grow-ing know-ing Je-sus when I work and when I play.
I am grow-ing know-ing Je-sus. I am grow-ing in His love.

© Karyn Henley. All rights reserved.

Playsongs Bible Time: Fours, Spring Quarter

Lesson 2

Jesus Does Amazing Things Called Miracles

Memory Verse for the Quarter: "Grow knowing Jesus." 2 Peter 3:18, ICB, simplified

Scripture "All the people were amazed." Matthew 12:23, ICB

Bible Story Jesus turns water into wine, John 2:1-11

Goal Learn that Jesus does amazing things we call miracles.

Today's Teacher Task
- Point out the things we call miracles.
- Repeat as often as appropriate:
  Jesus does amazing things.
  We call those amazing things "miracles."

INTRODUCTION

Materials: balloons, streamers, tape and/or plastic temporary adhesive (Plasti-Tak or Tak 'n Stik)

Do: As the children arrive, inflate the balloons and ask children to help hang the balloons and streamers up around the classroom to decorate it for a "wedding celebration."

Discuss: Ask the children to tell you about different types of parties they've had or attended. Ask them what they did at the party and what they like about parties. Say: **Jesus went to a party one time. Do you think he laughed and had fun?**

LARGE GROUP TIME

Sing "Come to the Circle" (page 6/track #9), and gather the children together in a large group.

Bible Story

Materials: a Bible with a bookmark at John 2, a plastic pitcher (preferably not transparent), a packet of pre-sweetened red or purple powdered drink mix, a long handled stirring spoon, water, a 2-cup lliquid measuring cup, paper cups, paper towels

Timesaver Option: the <u>Before I Dream Bedtime Bible Storybook</u> by Karyn Henley

Do: If you use the Bible storybook, read the story "Nothing Left to Drink."

Otherwise, before class, pour the powdered drink mix into the pitcher and note the amount of water you will need for it. In class, open the Bible to John 2 and say: **Here's where the Bible tells about Jesus going to a wedding party. Let's pretend we are at that wedding party.** Give each child an empty cup. **Let's pretend we've all had something to drink. But now our cups are empty. We want some more. That's what happened at the wedding party. The people had food to eat and wine to drink. But they ran out of drinks. The people wanted more. Jesus' mother went to him and said, "Jesus, they've run out of wine to drink!" Jesus saw some tall jars, like huge pitchers.** Hold the pitcher up. **He told the servants to fill the jars with water. So they did.** Put water into the measuring cup (use the amount recommended on the packet of drink mix.) Let the children look at the water. Say: **It's plain water, right? The servants put plain water into the jars.** Pour the water into the pitcher. Stir it. **The servants then dipped the water out to give it to the people to drink. And guess what?** Begin pouring the drink into each child's cup. **The water had turned into wine! Isn't that amazing? Jesus did amazing things. We call those amazing things "miracles."**

As the children drink, tell them how you turned the water into juice. Tell them you did a trick. But Jesus really made water turn into wine. It was not a trick. It was a true miracle.

Songs and Movement

Sing the memory verse song, "Growing Knowing Jesus" (page 6/track #28).

Sing the scripture for today, "All the people were amazed," to the tune of "Mary Had a Little Lamb" (track #2).
> **All the people were amazed,**
> **Were amazed, were amazed,**
> **All the people were amazed**
> **To see what Jesus did.**

Prayer
Ask the children to fold their hands and pray the words after you:
Dear God, Thank you that Jesus does amazing things called miracles. Amen.

EXPLORE-A-BINS
Choose from these activities. Use them in the order that best suits your needs.

1. The Art Bin: Sprinkle Pictures
Materials: newspapers or a plastic tablecloth, a bucket or tub or sink of water,

powdered <u>unsweetened</u> drink mix of a variety of colors, plastic picnic bowls, plastic spoons, paper towels

Do: Cover the work surface with newspaper or plastic tablecloth. Put a different color of drink mix into each bowl. Give each child a piece of paper. Help each child dip his paper into the water, then place it on the newspaper or tablecloth. Now give each child a spoon and ask the children to dip a little of one color of colored powder (drink mix) and sprinkle it on their paper. Then they can sprinkle other colors onto their papers. Then let this dry.

Discuss: As the children work, say, **We can make a white sheet of paper turn different colors with paint or this colored powder. Is that a miracle? Can we change the paper into something else completely different? That's what Jesus did to the water. What did He turn it into? Whose power did that? Jesus did amazing things. We call those amazing things "miracles."** Sing "All the People Were Amazed" (above) and "Growing Knowing Jesus" (page 6/track #28).

2. The Science-Math Bin: Making Butter

Materials: 1/2 cup of whipping cream, a 1-quart plastic jar with a tight-fitting lid, paper towels, crackers, salt, butter knife, spoon, hand wipes

Do: Ask the children to clean their hands with wipes. Let them look at the whipping cream and smell it. Then pour it into the jar and put the lid on. Let each child have a turn shaking the jar. Continue shaking the jar until butter forms. This will take about 5 minutes. Pour off the liquid. Add a little salt to the butter if you wish. Press the butter to squeeze out extra liquid. Pour that liquid off. Spread butter on crackers and eat.

Discuss: As the children shake the cream, ask them where cream comes from. Ask what can be made out of milk and cream. (Ice cream, butter, cheese, cottage cheese.) **God made cows and the milk and cream that comes from them. People take the milk and cream and make ice cream, butter, and cheese. But can people change milk into orange juice? Can they change it into grape juice? Can we look at cream and tell it to change into butter and it happens? But Jesus could do any of these things. We can shake and shake and shake and make butter. But we can't change milk or butter into a completely different kind of food. That's what Jesus did to the water. What did He turn it into? Whose power did that? Jesus did amazing things. We call those amazing things "miracles."** Sing "All the People Were Amazed" (page 8/track #2) and "Growing Knowing Jesus" (page 6/track #28).

3. The Look and Listen Bin: Growing

Materials: books, CDs and/or DVDs about Jesus, or about parties, or about food CD/DVD player

You may choose your own books and CDs/DVDs. Some suggestions are:

<u>Jesus Loves Me</u> by Debby Anderson
<u>Water, Water Everywhere</u> by Julie Aigner-Clark
<u>Do You Know About Water?</u> by Mae Blacker Freeman
<u>Spot Bakes a Cake</u> by Eric Hill
<u>Bear's All-Night Party</u> by Bill Harley
<u>Rabbit's Pajama Party</u> by Stuart J. Murphy
"The Birthday Song" and "God Made Food" from <u>PlaySongs: Grow, Grow, Grow</u> CD/DVD by Karyn Henley
"Stone Soup" from <u>PlaySongs: Tiny Treasures</u> CD/DVD by Karyn Henley
"Nothing Left to Drink" from the <u>Before I Dream Bedtime Bible Storybook</u> by Karyn Henley

Do: Read the book(s) to the children or let them look at the pictures, and ask them to describe the things in the books that show Jesus doing amazing things or parties or food. Listen to any CDs/DVDs you've chosen.

Discuss: Talk about the amazing things Jesus did. If you read or watch books/CDs/DVDs about parties, talk about the wedding party Jesus went to and what happened there. If you read or watch books/CDs/DVDs about food or water, talk about how Jesus changed water into wine. Say, **Jesus did amazing things. We call those amazing things "miracles."** Sing "All the People Were Amazed" (page 8/track #2) and "Growing Knowing Jesus" (page 6/track #28).

4. **The Creative Movement Bin: Still Water, Splash!**

    Materials: a blue sheet, towel, pillowcase, or scarf

    Do: Lay the blue fabric on the floor, bunched up to make a narrow "river." Encourage children to jump across from one side of the "river" to the other. Encourage them to join in the following:

<u>Still Water, Splash!</u>   (track #76)
   Still water. . .Still water. . .   (hold hands out, palms down, still)
   Still water. . .
   Splash!   (clap)

<u>This is the Way</u>   (to the tune of "Here We Go 'Round the Mulberry Bush"/track #87)
   This is the way we splash in the water,
      splash in the water, splash in the water,   (Pretend to splash.)
   This is the way we splash in the water,
      Thank you, God, for water.

   Other verses can be:
      This is the way we swim in the water. . .   (Pretend to swim.)
      This is the way we wash in the water. . .   (Pretend to bathe.)
      This is the way we drink the water. . .   (Pretend to drink.)
      This is the way we water the plants. . .   (Pretend to water plants.)

Discuss: Ask the children what happened to the water that was in the jars at the wedding party Jesus went to. Say: **Jesus did amazing things. We call those amazing things "miracles."** Sing "All the People Were Amazed" (page 8/track #2) and "Growing Knowing Jesus" (page 6/track #28).

5. The Game Bin: Change It

Materials: a basket or box, a towel or cloth that will cover the basket or box, a variety of household items that are familiar to four-year-olds (comb, CD, crayon, small cup, spoon, small toy, etc.)

Do: Fill the basket or box with six to eight items. Let the children look at the items. Then cover the items with the cloth. Choose one child to be the "Changer." Ask the other children to close and cover their eyes. Now ask the Changer to quietly remove one item from the basket. Set it aside somewhere the others can't see it. Then cover the items again. Ask the children to open their eyes. Take the cloth off and ask them to look at the items. Tell them that when they have figured out what the Changer did to change what was in the basket, they should raise their hands. Ask one of the children to say how the basket's contents have changed. That child can then become the Changer. You can also have the children change the contents by adding a new object.

Discuss: Ask, **How are we changing what's in the basket?** (By adding or removing objects.) **What did Jesus change at the wedding party? Jesus did amazing things. We call those amazing things "miracles."** Sing "All the People Were Amazed" (page 8/track #2) and "Growing Knowing Jesus" (page 6/track #28).

6. The Snack Bin: Lemonade

Materials: 5 medium-sized lemons, 5 cups cold water, 1 cup sugar, a knife for teacher's use, a pitcher, measuring cups and spoons, a long-handled spoon, paper cups, paper towels, hand wipes, optional: crackers

Do: Ask the children to clean their hands with wipes. Cut the lemons so each child can have a part of a lemon. Ask the children to squeeze a drop of their lemon onto one of their fingers and take a taste. Ask how it tastes. Then ask each child to squeeze his part of the lemon into the pitcher. Let the children help add the water and sugar. Let them take turns stirring the mixture. Then let them drink the lemonade and tell how it has changed from the drop of juice they tasted before.

Discuss: Ask the children to describe the differences in flavors. Ask them to tell how they helped change the pure lemon juice into something they could drink. Ask, **Did Jesus change water into wine by stirring some mix or juice into the water? No. The water just turned into wine all by itself because Jesus told it to. Whose power made the water change? Jesus did amazing things. We call those amazing things "miracles."** Sing "All the People Were Amazed" (page 8/track #2) and "Growing Knowing Jesus" (page 6/track #28).

Lesson 3

Jesus is a Good Friend

Memory Verse for the Quarter: "Grow knowing Jesus." 2 Peter 3:18, ICB, simplified

Scripture Jesus said, "Now you are my friends." John 15:15, NLT

Bible Story Jesus has dinner at Matthew's house, Matthew 9:9, 10

Goal Learn that Jesus spent time with his friends, and He spends time with us. Learn that Jesus is a good friend.

Today's Teacher Task
- Point out and describe good friends.
- Repeat as often as appropriate:
    Good friends spend time with us.
    They work with us and play with us.
    Jesus is with us when we work and play.
    Jesus is a good friend.

INTRODUCTION

Materials: boxes large enough for the children to sit in (or use classroom chairs), crayons, option: PlaySongs: Down By the Station CD and CD player

Do: As the children arrive, ask them to line up the boxes or chairs to make a train. If you use boxes, ask the children to color the sides of this box train. If you use chairs, ask the children to make the train by setting two chairs side by side, then two more behind it, and so on, so that each section of the train has a place for two friends to sit next to each other. Sing "Down by the Station." If you've chosen to use the CD, play the song. You may also want to pretend that the boxes are cars, trucks, etc. as you play "Red Says Stop" from the same CD.

Discuss: Talk about going places with friends. If two children get into the same box or color the same box, talk about how they are friends. Ask where they might go with friends.

LARGE GROUP TIME
Sing "Come to the Circle" (page 6/track #9), and gather the children together in a large group.

Bible Story

   Materials: a Bible with a bookmark at Matthew 9

Do: In class, ask the children to sit in a circle. Open the Bible to Matthew 9 and say: **Here's where the Bible tells about Jesus and a man named Matthew.** Set the Bible aside. To tell the story, play a game.
Walk around the circle, saying:

One day Jesus saw someone named Matthew. (Stand still behind a child.)
Jesus said, "Matthew, come with me." (Tap the child and have her follow you.)
Jesus went to Matthew's house for dinner. (Stop at the child's original place.)
Lots of people came to eat with them. (Ask the rest of the children to pretend to eat.)
Jesus had lots of friends. (Motion toward all the children.)

Now the child who was Matthew walks around the circle and taps another on the head as you repeat the story.

Say: **Good friends spend time with us. They work with us and play with us. Jesus is with us when we work and play. Jesus is a good friend.**

Songs and Movement
Sing the memory verse song, "Growing Knowing Jesus" (page 6/track #28).

Sing the scripture for today to the tune of "The Farmer in the Dell" (track #60).
**"Now you are my friends, Now you are my friends."
Jesus has said to us, "Now you are my friends."**

Prayer
Ask the children to fold their hands and pray the words after you:
Dear God, Thank you that Jesus is our friend. Amen.

EXPLORE-A-BINS
Choose from these activities. Use them in the order that best suits your needs.

1. The Art Bin: Bandanas

Materials: newspapers or a plastic tablecloth, one white handkerchief for each child, fabric paints or markers

Do: Cover the work surface with newspaper or a tablecloth. Give each child a handkerchief. Ask the children to paint designs on the handkerchiefs. Encourage each child to think of a friend they can give the bandana to.

Discuss: Ask, **What do friends do with you? What did Jesus do with his friend Matthew? Sometimes friends give things to each other. What does Jesus give to you? Good friends spend time with us. They work with us and play with us. Jesus is with us when we work and play. Jesus is a good friend.** Sing "Now You Are My Friends" (page 13/track #60).

© Karyn Henley. All rights reserved.

2. The Science-Math Bin: Map to My Friend's House

Materials: large pieces of manila paper, two small boxes for each child (single-serving milk cartons, cereal boxes, juice boxes, or yogurt containers work well), glue or tape or plastic temporary adhesive (Plasti-Tak or Tak 'n Stik), crayons, a ruler, optional: small toy vehicles

Do: Give each child a piece of paper and two small boxes. Ask the children to draw a street on the paper, then use glue, tape, or plastic adhesive to stick one box on each end of the road. One box represents the child's house. The other represent's a friend's. Children can draw grass and trees on the paper. They can measure the distance betwen houses and drive toy cars from one house to the other.

Discuss: Ask, **Do you have friends who live near you? How do you get to your friends' houses? Do you ever eat at a friend's house? Whose house did Jesus go to for dinner? Good friends spend time with us. They work with us and play with us. Jesus is with us when we work and play. Jesus is a good friend.** Sing "Now You Are My Friends" (page 13/track #60).

3. The Look and Listen Bin: Friends

Materials: books, CDs and/or DVDs about friends, CD/DVD player

You may choose your own books and CDs/DVDs. Some suggestions are:
The Rainbow Fish by Marcus Pfister   Stone Soup by Marcia Brown
My Friend and I by Lisa Jahn-Clough   The Mitten by Alvin Tresselt
Bear's Busy Family by Stella Blackstone   Friends by Helme Heine
Where are Maisy's Friends? by Lucy Cousins
Alfie Gives a Hand by Shirley Hughes
Will I Have a Friend by Miriam Cohen
Dear God, Thank You for Friends by Annie Fitzgerald & Ken Abraham
"Friends" and "Stone Soup" from PlaySongs: Tiny Treausres CD/DVD by Karyn Henley
"I'm a Helper" and "Mess in the Bedroom" from PlaySongs: Grow, Grow, Grow
    CD/DVD by Karyn Henley

Do: Read the book(s) or let the children look at the pictures while you point out friends. Play any CDs or DVDs you've chosen, and describe friends.

Discuss: Say, **Good friends spend time with us. They work with us and play with us. Jesus is with us when we work and play. Jesus is a good friend.**

4. The Creative Movement Bin: Jesus is My Best Friend

Materials: none

Do: Encourage the children to copy you as you do the following action songs.

<u>Jesus is My Best Friend</u>   (to the tune of "Polly Put the Kettle On"/track #49)

Jesus is my best friend,	(shake hands with each other)
Jesus is my best friend,	
Jesus is my best friend all day long.	(arms overhead in circle for a sun)

Keep the first three lines and change the last line as you sing other verses:

. . .**all night long**	(close eyes, place head on hands)
. . .**when it's cold**	(rub arms and shiver)
. . .**when it's hot**	(wipe forehead with hand)
. . .**all the time**	(hold arms out wide)

<u>Skip Along</u>   (to the tune of "Row, Row, Row Your Boat"/track #75)
**Skip*, skip, skip along.
This is what I know:
Jesus is my special friend
Everywhere I go.**

*Let the children suggest other movements to do as you continue the song.

Discuss: Say, **Good friends spend time with us. They work with us and play with us. Jesus is with us when we work and play. Jesus is a good friend.**

5. The Game Bin: Around the World

Materials: magazine pictures of a variety of nature scenes, a box or bag

Do: Put the magazine pictures into the box or bag. Let each child take a turn closing his eyes and pulling out a picture. The child shows his picture to everyone. Then lead the children in pretending you are in that place, traveling across the land or sea. For example: "We are going to climb this mountain. It's very high. Up we go. Up and up and up." Pretend to climb, sail the seas, hike across the fields, etc.

Discuss: Ask, **Is Jesus with you in a place like this? Jesus goes with us everywhere. Good friends spend time with us. They work with us and play with us. Jesus is with us when we work and play. Jesus is a good friend.** Sing "Now You Are My Friends" (page 13/track #60).

6. The Snack Bin: Sharing with a Friend

Materials: apple slices, cheese slices, juice, paper plates and cups, paper towels, hand wipes

Do: Ask the children to wash their hands with wipes. Pray, thanking God for Jesus and for the snack. Serve two or three slices of apple and cheese to each child and encourage each child to give (share) one of his slices to the child next to him.

Discuss: Talk about how the children in class are friends. Ask, **What do good friends do with each other? How do good friends treat each other? Good friends spend time with us. They work with us and play with us. Jesus is with us when we work and play. Jesus is a good friend.** Sing "Now You Are My Friends" (page 13/track #60).

Lesson 4

Jesus is a Teacher

> **Memory Verse for the Quarter:** "Grow knowing Jesus." 2 Peter 3:18, ICB, simplified
>
> **Scripture** "Jesus taught the people." Matthew 5:2, ICB
>
> **Bible Story** Jesus teaches on the mountain, Matthew 5, 6
>
> **Goal** Learn that Jesus is a teacher. He teaches us God's ways.
> Learn that Jesus taught us not to worry, because God will take care of us.
>
> **Today's Teacher Task**
> - Point out things Jesus taught.
> - Repeat as often as appropriate:
>   **Jesus is a teacher.
>   He teaches us God's ways.
>   He taught us not to worry,
>   because God will take care of us.**

INTRODUCTION

Materials: play dough*, paper plates, small rocks/gravel/sand, small twigs and plant stems with small leaves

*To make play dough, mix 1 part water, 1 part salt, and 3 parts flour.

Do: As the children arrive, give each of them a paper plate and some play dough. Ask the children to make mountains out of the dough. Then ask them to press rocks, gravel, and/or sand into the sides of their mountains. Ask them to stick twigs and stems with leaves into the sides of the mountains to make trees.

Discuss: Ask: **Have you ever been to the mountains? What are mountains like? What did you do in the mountains?** (Or if you live in the mountains, ask, "If someone had never seen the mountains before, how would you describe the mountains to them? What would you show them if they came to see you?") **Who made mountains? What do you like about mountains?**

LARGE GROUP TIME
Sing "Come to the Circle" (page 6/track #9), and gather the children together in a large group.

Bible Story

Materials: a Bible with a bookmark at Matthew 6, birds made according to the pattern and instructions on page 22, string, tape, flowers (real or artificial), one or more vases

Timesaver Option: the Before I Dream Bedtime Bible Storybook and/or the Before I Dream: In Jesus' Arms CD, a CD player

Do: If you use the Bible storybook and/or CD, read the story "Ravens and Lilies" or play it on CD. Listen to "Look at All God Made," the song that follows the story on CD.

If you do not use the storybook or CD, before class, make the birds as shown on the pattern page and hang them up from the ceiling or window sill or doorway in the classroom. If you use artificial flowers, set them here and there around the story area. If you use real flowers, set one or more vases out with the flowers in them.

In class, open the Bible to Matthew 6 and say: **Here's where the Bible tells about a time when Jesus' followers listened to him teach.** Set the Bible aside, and ask the children to follow you as you walk around the room. Say: **One day Jesus took his friends up onto a mountain.** Lead the childrent to pretend to be walking up a mountainside. **Then Jesus sat down.** Ask the children to sit. **And Jesus taught them. He said, "Look at the flowers."** Let the children smell the flowers as you talk. **Do they make their own clothes?** Let the children answer. **But they are beautiful. God takes care of the flowers and makes them beautiful. Jesus also said, "Look at the birds."** Blow on the birds so they will "fly" around on their strings. **Do they plant seeds and grow food like a farmer does?** Let the children answer. **God takes care of them and gives them the food they need. Jesus said, "If God takes care of birds and flowers, you can be sure He will take care of you."**

Say: **Jesus is a teacher. He teaches us God's ways. He taught us not to worry, because God will take care of us.**

Songs and Movement

Sing the memory verse song, "Growing Knowing Jesus" (page 6/track #28).
Play or sing the song "Look at the Flowers" from the book/cassette/CD My First Hymnal
   by Karyn Henley, Dennas Davis, and Randall Dennis
Sing "Do Not Worry" to the tune of "Mary Had a Little Lamb" (track #12):
   "Do not worry," Jesus said,
   Jesus said, Jesus said,
   "Do not worry," Jesus said,
   "God takes care of you."

Prayer

Ask the children to fold their hands and pray the words after you:
   Dear God, Thank you that Jesus is a good teacher. Amen.

EXPLORE-A-BINS
Choose from these activities. Use them in the order that best suits your needs.

1. The Art Bin: Jelly Bean Nest

Materials: paper plates, glue, shredded coconut, yellow food coloring, jelly beans or speckled "bird's egg" candies, mixing bowl, mixing spoon, paper towels, hand wipes

Do: Give each child a piece of paper. Ask children to help you prepare the coconut "straw": Dump the coconut into the bowl. Add yellow food coloring and mix. Now ask the children to make a circle of glue about the size of a baseball on their paper. They sprinkle yellow coconut onto the glue to make the nest. Then they glue jelly beans or "bird's egg" candies in the coconut nest.

Discuss: Ask: **Did you ever see a bird's nest? What was it like? Why do birds build nests? Where else might birds live? Do you have a pet bird or know someone who does? What is the bird like? What kinds of birds do you see where you live? What did Jesus teach us to think about when we see birds?** Say: **Jesus is a teacher. He teaches us God's ways. He taught us not to worry, because God will take care of us.** Sing "Do Not Worry" (page 18/track #12).

2. The Science-Math Bin: Taking Care of Plants

Materials: newspaper or plastic tablecloth, two small plants in pots, paper towels, paper, crayons

Do: Ask the children to describe the plants or point to the plant's leaves, stem, and flowers if there are any. Tell the children that the flowers are the parts of the plant that make new seeds to plant for next year. The leaves gather sunlight and make the plant's food. The stem brings water into the plant from the ground. Now ask each child to gently pull up on one of the plants so that it comes out of the pot and you can see the roots. Tell the children that the roots soak up water from the ground and take it to the stem. Roots also hold the plant in the ground when the wind blows. If you have other groups, repot the uprooted plant.

Now give each child a piece of paper. Ask the children to draw the plant and its roots.

Discuss: Ask: **What does a plant need in order to grow? What do we call people who take care of plants?** (farmers, gardeners, nursery workers) **What did Jesus teach people to think about when they see flowers?** Say: **Jesus is a teacher. He teaches us God's ways. He taught us not to worry, because God will take care of us.** Sing "Do Not Worry" (page 18/track #12).

© Karyn Henley. All rights reserved.

3. The Look and Listen Bin: Plants and Birds

Materials: books, CDs/DVDs about plants and birds, a CD/DVD player

You may use your own books and CDs/DVDs. The following are suggestions:
<u>Are You My Mother?</u> by P.D. Eastman
<u>The Carrot Seed</u> by Ruth Krauss
<u>Make Way for Ducklings</u> by Robert McCloskey
<u>The Story about Ping</u> by Flack and Wiese
<u>Planting a Rainbow</u> by Lois Ehlert
<u>Growing Vegetable Soup</u> by Lois Ehlert
<u>This Year's Garden</u> by Cynthis Rylant
<u>From Seed to Plant</u> by Gail Gibbons
<u>7 Days of Creation</u> by Mindy MacDonald
<u>The Little Duck</u> by Judy Dunn
<u>About Birds: A Guide for Children</u> by Cathryn Sill
<u>Tell Me About God</u> by Karyn Henley
"Look At the Flowers" (Matthew 6) from <u>My First Hymnal</u> CD by Karyn Henley
"It's A Beautiful World," on <u>PlaySongs: Down By the Station</u> CD/DVD by Karyn Henley
"I Like," on <u>PlaySongs: Noah's Zoo</u> CD/DVD by Karyn Henley
"The Seed Song," on <u>PlaySongs: Grow,Grow, Grow</u> CD/DVD by Karyn Henley
"Daffy Daffodils," on <u>PlaySongs: Tiny Treausres</u> CD/DVD by Karyn Henley

Do: Read the book(s) and/or play the CD/DVD. Point out the plants, flowers, and birds.

Discuss: Ask: **What did Jesus teach us about plants and birds?** Say: **Jesus is a teacher. He teaches us God's ways. He taught us not to worry, because God will take care of us.**

4. The Creative Movement Bin: Plants and Animals

Materials: optional: CDs/DVDs with animal songs, CD/DVD player
CD/DVD Suggestions:
"Froggie Jump" from <u>Playsongs: Down By the Station</u> by Karyn Henley
"The Mice Go Tiptoe" song <u>Playsongs: I Feel Like a Giggle</u> by Karyn Henley
"God Made the Earth" from <u>PlaySongs: Five Little Ladybugs</u>
"Tall Tall Tree," from <u>PlaySongs: Grow, Grow, Grow</u>

Do: Play the CD/DVD and ask the children to do the actions to the songs. And/or encourage the children to copy you in the following action rhymes/songs.

<u>Birdies Fly</u> (to the tune of "This Old Man"/track #4)

Birdies fly, birdies fly,	(stand and pretend to fly)
Fly across the great blue sky	
With a flutter, flutter, flap-a-flap-a-flap	
Find your nest and take a nap.	(sit, head on hands as if sleeping)

<u>This is the Way</u>   (to the tune of "Here We Go 'Round the Mulberry Bush")

**This is the way we plant the seeds,
   plant the seeds, plant the seeds,**   (Pretend to plant seeds.)
**This is the way we plant the seeds,
   Thank you, God, for seeds.**

Other verses can be:
This is the way we water the seeds. . .   (Pretend to water seeds.)
This is the way we pull the weeds. . .   (Pretend to pull weeds.)
This is the way the sun shines down. . .   (Pretend to be the sun shining.)
This is the way the plant grows tall. . .   (Squat; then stand up slowly.)

<u>Dig a Small Garden</u>   (to the tune of "Rock–a–Bye Baby"/track #11)
Before you teach the song, explain what a "bouquet" is.

Dig a small garden,	(pretend to dig)
Plant little seeds.	(pretend to plant seeds)
Sprinkle with water,	(pretend to water the seeds)
Pull up the weeds.	(pretend to pull weeds)
Let the sun shine down	(arms in circle like a sun)
Every day.	
Soon there'll be flowers	(arms together, fingers spread)
For my bouquet.	(Fold hands and say "Thank you, God.")

Discuss: Ask: **What did Jesus teach us about plants and birds?** Say: **Jesus is a teacher. He teaches us God's ways. He taught us not to worry, because God will take care of us.**

5. The Game Bin: Flowers in the Wind

Materials: none

Do: Ask the children to stand and spread out. Then ask them to pretend they are flowers, rooted in the ground. Point out the colors of the flowers (by the colors of clothes they are wearing). Then tell the children you will be the wind. When you say, "*Breezy*," they should sway slowly and gently. When you say, "*Windy*," they sway faster and deeper, back and forth, remembering to stay rooted in the ground. When you say, "*Hurricane!*" they all fall down. Vary between "*Breezy*" and "*Windy*" several times. Then suddenly say, "*Hurricane!*"

Discuss: Ask: **What holds flowers in the ground? What else do roots do for a flower?** (brings water into the flower from the ground) **What did Jesus want us to remember when we see flowers?** Say: **Jesus is a teacher. He teaches us God's ways. He taught us not to worry, because God will take care of us.** Sing "Do Not Worry" (page 18/track #12).

6. The Snack Bin: Plant and Bird Snack

Materials: carrot sticks, apple slices, boiled eggs, juice, knife for teacher, paper plates and cups, paper towels, hand wipes

Do: Ask the children to clean their hands with wipes. Give each child a paper plate and some carrot sticks and apple slices. Ask the children what plants each of these comes from. Show the children the boiled eggs. Ask what kind of bird it comes from. Let the children watch you slice the boiled eggs. Give them some of the egg slices to eat.

Discuss: Ask: **What did Jesus teach us about plants and birds?** Say: **Jesus is a teacher. He teaches us God's ways. He taught us not to worry, because God will take care of us.** Sing "Do Not Worry" (page 18/track #12).

Playsongs Bible Time: Fours, Spring Quarter   23

Bird Pattern and Instructions

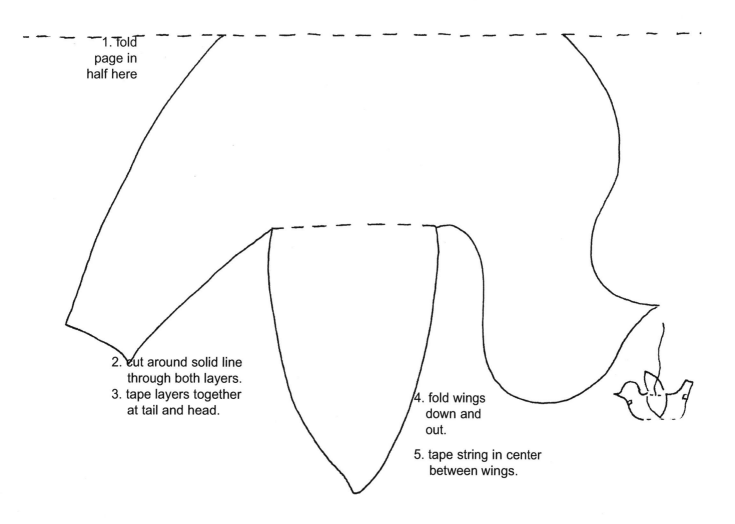

1. fold page in half here
2. cut around solid line through both layers.
3. tape layers together at tail and head.
4. fold wings down and out.
5. tape string in center between wings.

Lesson 5

Jesus is Like a Good Shepherd

Memory Verse for the Quarter: "Grow knowing Jesus." 2 Peter 3:18, ICB, simplified

Scripture Jesus said, "I am the good shepherd. I know my own sheep."
John 10:14, NLT

Bible Story Jesus is our good shepherd, John 10:1-16, Psalm 23, Luke 15:3-7

Goal Learn that Jesus is like a good shepherd to us. He takes care of us.

Today's Teacher Task
- Point out things show Jesus' care.
- Repeat as often as appropriate:
  Jesus is like a good shepherd to us.
  He takes care of us.

INTRODUCTION

Materials: blocks, cotton balls, ten index cards, marker

Do: Before class, write the numerals 1 through 10 on the index cards, one numeral on each card. As the children arrive, ask them to build ten sheep pens out of blocks. Then in each pen, place one of the cards. Now ask the children to place in each pen the number of cotton balls that matches the numeral on the card in that pen. When the children have finished, and if you have time, ask them to give you each of the cards. Lay the cards on floor or table so the children can see the numerals. Then take one cotton ball out of the pen that has 10 sheep in it. Ask a child to place the correct card in that pen. Continue taking away one sheep from each pen in random order, and asking the children to place the correct cards in each pen. You can also add sheep to pens.

Discuss: Ask the children if they've ever seen real sheep. Ask them what sheep are like. Ask: **Who takes care of sheep? Why would sheep need somebody to take care of them?**

LARGE GROUP TIME
Sing "Come to the Circle" (page 6/track #9), and gather the children together in a large group.

Bible Story

Materials: a Bible with a bookmark at John 10

Timesaver Option: the <u>Before I Dream Bedtime Bible Storybook</u> and/or the <u>Before I Dream: Dream of Heaven</u> CD, CD player

Do: If you choose to use the Bible storybook, read "Sheep and Shepherd" or play it on CD. Play "The Lord is My Sheperd," the song that follows the story on CD.

If you choose not to use the Bible storybook or CD, in class open the Bible to John 10 and say: **Here's where the Bible tells us that Jesus is like a good shepherd to us.** Ask the children to pretend they are sheep. Walk around among the "sheep," patting each of them as you say, **A good shepherd takes care of his sheep. He takes them to get water to drink and grass to eat. He keeps them healthy and safe. One day Jesus told a story about a good shepherd who had one hundred sheep. At night, he counted them to make sure they had all come home.** Count the children. Then ask one of them to hide while everyone else closes their eyes. Count them again. **One night when the shepherd counted, he found that one sheep was missing.** Ask one child to be the shepherd. Ask the hiding child to say, "Baa." The shepherd can then find his lost sheep and bring him back. **The good shepherd looked and looked for his sheep. At last he found the lost sheep. He brought him back home and took care of him.**

Say: **Jesus is like a good shepherd to us. He takes care of us. How does Jesus take care of us?**

Songs and Movement

Sing the memory verse song, "Growing Knowing Jesus" (page 6/track #28).
Sing the first two verses of "Mary Had a Little Lamb," substituting "The Shepherd" instead of "Mary" (track #31).
    For the third verse, sing: **I am Jesus' little lamb, little lamb, little lamb,**
                                     I am Jesus' little lamb; I follow Him each day.

Prayer

Ask the children to fold their hands and pray the words after you:
    Dear God, Thank you that Jesus is our Good Shepherd and takes care of us.
                                                                 Amen.

EXPLORE-A-BINS
Choose from these activities. Use them in the order that best suits your needs.

1. **The Art Bin: Paper Plate Sheep**

   Materials: white paper plates, crayons or markers, two sheep ears for each child (copied and cut out from page 29), tape or stapler and staples, glue, cotton balls

   Do: Give each child a paper plate. Ask the children to draw a sheep face on the plate. Then give each of them two sheep ears, and ask them to tape or staple the ears in place on the plate. Bend the wide side of the ears forward. Now ask the children to glue cotton balls around the perimeter of the plate.

   Discuss: Ask: **Why do sheep need a shepherd? Why do we need Jesus to take care of us? How does Jesus take care of us?** Say: **Jesus is like a good shepherd to us.** Sing "The Shepherd Had a Little Lamb" (page 25/track #31).

2. **The Science-Math Bin: Will It Last?**

   Materials: a pillowcase or grocery bag, a variety of objects that can be handled by children (These should be objects that do not last a long time: a banana, balloon, toy, sock, toothbrush, paper, toothpaste, plastic spoon, candle, etc.)

   Do: Before class, put the objects into the pillowcase or bag. In class, ask each child to take a turn pulling an item out of the bag. As each item is pulled out, ask: **Will this last forever? Why not?**

   Discuss: Say: **Will Jesus' love for you last forever? Yes! Jesus will never stop loving you. Jesus is like a good shepherd to us. He takes care of us. How does Jesus take care of us?** Sing "The Shepherd Had a Little Lamb" (page 25/track #31).

3. **The Look and Listen Bin: Sheep and the Good Shepherd**

   Materials: books and/or CDs/DVDs about sheep or Jesus' love and care, CD/DVD player

   You may choose your own books and CDs/DVDs. Some suggestions are:

   Jesus Loves Me, Jesus Loves the Little Children, or Jesus is With Me by
       Debby Anderson
   Sheep in a Jeep, Sheep in a Shop, Sheep in a Ship, or Sheep Takes a Hike by
       Nancy E. Shaw
   "I Am Your God," from PlaySongs: Noah's Zoo CD/DVD by Karyn Henley
   "God Will Never Stop Loving Me" from PlaySongs: I Feel Like a Giggle CD/DVD by
       Karyn Henley

© Karyn Henley. All rights reserved.

"God's With Me" song from <u>My Thank You Bible Stories & Songs CD</u> by Karyn Henley
"Sheep and Shepherd" and "The Lord is My Shepherd" from <u>Before I Dream: Dream of Heaven</u> CD by Karyn Henley

Do: Read the book(s) to the children or let them look at the pictures, and/or listen to the songs on CD/DVD. Point out the sheep and/or Jesus' love and care.

Discuss: Say: **Jesus is like a good shepherd to us. He takes care of us. How does Jesus take care of us?**

4. The Creative Movement Bin: Jesus Takes Care of Me
   Materials: optional: <u>PlaySongs: Five Little Ladybugs</u> CD/DVD by Karyn Henley, CD/DVD player

   Do: Play the "Baby Bear Story" from the CD/DVD and ask the children to do the hand motions to the story. And/or encourage the children to join you in the following active rhymes or songs.

<u>I Have a Little Car</u>   (track #32)

I have a little car.	(pretend to drive)
It goes fast and slow.	(go fast and slow)
And God is with me everywhere	
I go, go, go.	
Stop!	(everybody freeze)
I have a little truck.	(pretend to drive)
It goes fast and slow.	(go fast and slow)
And God is with me everywhere	
I go, go, go.	
Stop!	(everybody freeze)

Continue by asking the children to suggest types of vehicles.

<u>Jesus Will Take Care of Me</u>   (to the tune of "London Bridge"/track #54)
Ask two children to form a bridge by facing each other and holding their hands up together. The other children go under this bridge until the word "Shepherd." Then the bridge comes down around the child who is under it at that time. Sing the next verse with that child's name in it.

Jesus will take care of me,	**Jesus will take care of _____.**
Care of me, care of me.	**Care of _____, Care of _____.**
Jesus will take care of me.	**Jesus will take care of _____.**
He's the Good Shepherd.	**He's the Good Shepherd.**

© Karyn Henley. All rights reserved.

Discuss: Ask: **What is a sheep like? What does a shepherd do?** Say: **Jesus is like a good shepherd to us. He takes care of us. How does Jesus take care of us?**

5. The Game Bin: Sheep Over the Fence

Materials: a jump rope

Do: Hold one end of the rope, and ask a helper to hold the other end. Hold the rope taut about 2-inches off the floor. Ask the children to pretend to be sheep jumping over the fence. Each child has a turn to jump over the jump-rope "fence." After all have jumped over, raise the fence about an inch. Ask the children to jump over again. Continue until the height is too great. Then the sheep can crawl under the fence.

Discuss: Ask: **What is a sheep like? What does a shepherd do?** Say: **Jesus is like a good shepherd to us. He takes care of us. How does Jesus take care of us?** Sing "The Shepherd Had a Little Lamb" (page 25/track #31).

6. The Snack Bin: Protective Shells

Materials: some peanuts in the shell, 2 cups shelled roasted peanuts, 1/2 tsp. salt, 1 Tbs. peanut oil, crackers, a blender, mixing bowl, mixing spoon, measuring cups and spoons, paper plates and cups, juice, paper towels, hand wipes

Do: Ask the children to examine the peanuts in the shell. Crack some open to see inside. Then ask the children to help measure and mix the ingredients as you make peanut butter. Grind the peanuts in the blender, 1/2 cup at a time. Put the ground peanuts in a bowl. Add peanut oil and salt. Stir well. Put the peanut mixture back into the blender, one cup at a time, adding a few drops of oil if necessary. Blend the peanut mixture until smooth. Then spread it on crackers.

Discuss: Ask: **What covers the peanut while it's growing under the ground?** (the shell). **How does the shell protect the peanut? What does protect mean? Who protects you or takes care of you? A good shepherd protects his sheep. Jesus is like a good shepherd to us. He takes care of us. How does Jesus take care of us?** Sing "The Shepherd Had a Little Lamb" (page 25/track #31).

Sheep Ears Pattern

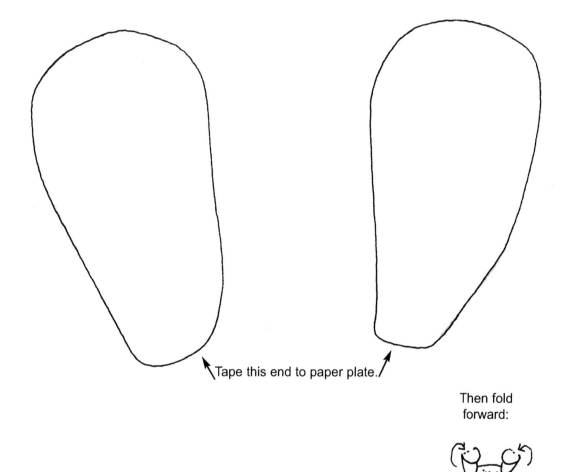

Tape this end to paper plate.

Then fold forward:

Lesson 6

Palm Sunday: Jesus is Our King

Memory Verse for the Quarter: "Grow knowing Jesus." 2 Peter 3:18, ICB, simplified

Scripture   "Praise to God in heaven!" Matthew 21:9, ICB

Bible Story   Jesus enters Jerusalem, Matthew 21:7-9

Goal   Learn that Jesus is our King.
                Learn that one way to treat Jesus as King is to praise Him.

Today's Teacher Task
- Point out and describe praise.
- Repeat as often as appropriate:
  Jesus is our King.
  We show He is our King by praising Him.

INTRODUCTION

Materials: paper lunch sacks, uncooked dry rice, paper clips, dried beans, pennies, cotton balls, salt, a stapler and staples, wide plastic tape (any color), a CD of praise music

Do: As the children arrive, ask them to help you make "shakers." Help them put the same amount of rice in two paper sacks, paper clips in two sacks, dried beans in two sacks, pennies in two sacks, cotton balls in two sacks, and salt in two sacks. Children can work with partners. One child holds the sack open, the other puts the materials into the sack. Then fold the tops of the sacks over several times. Staple them closed, and tape over the staples. You will use these "shakers" in the science-math activity. For now, let the children shake them as rhythm instruments to accompany the CD while marching around the room.

Discuss: Ask the children if they've ever played rhythm instruments before (drums, xylophone, sticks, cymbals, maracas, etc.). Tell them these shakers are rhythm instruments. Ask: **What part of yourself can be a rhythm instrument?** (hands that clap, feet that tap) Say: **We can praise God with rhythm instruments.**

LARGE GROUP TIME
Sing "Come to the Circle" (page 6/track #9), and gather the children together in a large group.

Bible Story

Materials: a Bible with a bookmark at Matthew 21, one palm leaf cut out of green paper for each child, and one for yourself (pattern on page 36)

Do: Open the Bible to Matthew 21 and say, **Here's where the Bible tells about a very special day when Jesus rode a donkey into the big city of Jerusalem.** Set the Bible aside. **People were so happy to see Jesus, they waved big leaves and said, "Hosanna! Jesus is coming!"** Give each child a palm leaf and ask them to follow you around the room and copy you as you say (track #48),

Jesus came riding on a donkey,	(Gallop.)
Riding, riding.	
The people said, "Hosanna!	(Stop and wave the leaves.)
Here comes the King!"	

Repeat this several times as you move around the room.

Say: **Jesus is our King. We show He is our King by praising Him.**

Songs and Movement

Sing the memory verse song, "Growing Knowing Jesus" (page 6/track #28).
March around the room, clapping and singing "Sing Hosanna!" (to the tune of "Are You Sleeping?"/track #74)):
Sing hosanna! Sing hosanna!
To the king! To the King!
We-ee love you, Jesus!
We know you're the King of
Everything! Everything!

Prayer

Ask the children to fold their hands and pray the words after you:
Dear God, Thank you that Jesus is our King. Amen.

EXPLORE-A-BINS
Choose from these activities. Use them in the order that best suits your needs.

1. The Art Bin: Cup Donkeys

Materials: one white styrene "hot" cup for each child, brown crayons, black permanent markers, glue, one or two paper plates, brown construction paper donkey ears*

Do: Before class, "donkey ears" (*triangles about the size shown). In class, give each child a cup. Help the children make an eye on each side and a nose on the bottom of the cup, as shown, by pressing the tip of a permanent against the cup. Ask the children to color the cup brown. Give each of them two donkey ears. Pour a puddle of glue onto the paper plate and show the children how to touch the lower side of each ear to the glue, then press the ears onto their cups.

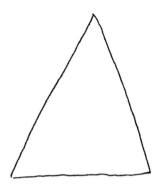
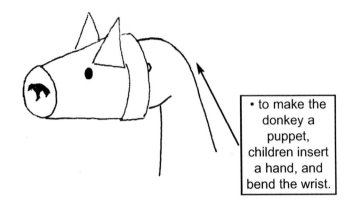

- to make the donkey a puppet, children insert a hand, and bend the wrist.

Discuss: As the children work, ask: **Who rode a donkey in our story? What did the people do when they found out Jesus was coming? Why? Why did they call Jesus the King?** (A king is in charge. He's the boss. The people were saying they wanted Jesus to be in charge of their lives.) Why is Jesus our King? (He is in charge of our lives.) Say: **Jesus is our King. We show He is our King by praising Him.** Sing "Sing Hosanna" (page 31/track #74).

2. The Science-Math Bin: Lunch Bag Shakers

Materials: lunch bag shakers from the introductory activity (If you did not do the introductory activity, children may do that activity at this time, and then move into the following. Or you can make the shakers before class.)

Do: Hand out the bags, one to each child. If you have fewer children than bags, place the remaining bags in the center of the group. If you have more children than bags, pair the children up in groups of two and give one bag to each couple. Ask one child to shake his bag. Ask the children to describe the sound. Then go around the group, asking each child to shake and listen to their bags, trying to find the one that matches. When you find a match, place the two bags aside. Go to the next child and ask her to shake her bag. Ask if the sound is louder or softer than the first. Then try to find a match for her bag. Continue until all bags have been matched. If you still have time, you may ask the children to march around the room with their shakers, singing, "Sing Hosanna" (page 31/track #74).

Discuss: Tell the children that their ears have tiny drums inside. Sound goes into their ears and hits the drum, causing it to shake (vibrate). Different sounds cause different vibrations. We then hear the sounds. Ask: **What sounds do you think Jesus heard when he rode the donkey into Jerusalem?** (palm leaves waving, donkey clopping, people shouting) What did the people say? Say: **Jesus is our King. We show He is our King by praising Him.** Sing "Sing Hosanna" (page 31/track #74).

3. The Look and Listen Bin: Praise

Materials: books and/or CDs/DVDs about Palm Sunday, Easter, praise and singing, CD/DVD player

You may use your own books and CDs/DVDs. The following are suggestions:
"L-O-V-E" from PlaySongs: Five Little Ladybugs CD/DVD by Karyn Henley
L-O-V-E, a PlaySongs book about Jesus' death and resurrection by Karyn Henley
"Praise Him, Praise Him" from PlaySongs: Tiny Treasures CD/DVD by Karyn Henley
"I Got Shoes," "Thank You, God, for Me" from PlaySongs: Noah's Zoo CD/DVD by Karyn Henley
Hurry, Hurry! by Mary Manz Simon   Easter ABC's by Isabel Anders
Little Colt's Palm Sunday by Michelle Medlock Adams
The Story of Easter by Aileen Fisher   J is for Jesus by Debbie Trafton O'Neal
My First Hymnal, CD by Karyn Henley

Do: Read the book(s) or let the children look at the pictures while you point out anything that has to do with Palm Sunday or Easter or praising God. Play any CDs or DVDs that you've chosen

Discuss: Say: **Jesus is our King. We show He is our King by praising Him.**

4. The Creative Movement Bin: Active Songs

Materials: rhythm instruments from the introductory activity, CDs/DVDs to sing and play along with, CD/DVD player

CD/DVD Suggestions:
"I Like to Play Music," from PlaySongs: Noah's Zoo by Karyn Henley
"Psalm 150," from PlaySongs: Five Little Ladybugs by Karyn Henley
"Rock-a-My Soul" and "Thank You March" from PlaySongs: I Feel Like a Giggle by Karyn Henley

Do: Encourage the children to play their instruments as you sing together or play the songs from the CDs/DVDs.

If you prefer not to use recorded music, you can sing "Sing Hosanna" (page 31/track #74), and "Praise to God" (page 31), and/or you can sing the following songs as the children march, clap, and play rhythm instruments.

Joyful Noise   (to the tune of "Oh Where Have You Been, Billy Boy?"/track #56)

**Oh, make a joyful noise to the Lord, all the earth,
Oh, make a joyful noise to the Lord.
Oh, make a joyful noise
All you girls and all you boys,
Oh, come make a joyful, joyful noise.**

<u>Marching, Marching</u>   (to the tune of "Twinkle, Twinkle, Little Star"/track #58)

**Marching, marching, everyone,
Marching, marching, here we come.
We love Jesus; He's our King,
He is why we march and sing.
Marching, marching, everyone,
Marching, marching, here we come.**

Discuss: Say: **Jesus is our King. We show He is our King by praising Him.**

5. The Game Bin: Tiptoe Praise

Materials: a paper palm leaf for each child (from story time)

Do: Give each child a palm leaf. Sing "Praise to God " (page 35/track #65) or "Sing Hosanna" (page 31/track #74) while the children dance around the room. Instruct them to stop and sit wherever they are when you stop singing. They should also be very quiet. Now tiptoe around the room, touching one child's head at a time. When a child is touched, he must follow you, tiptoeing quietly. When all children are following you, start the game over with singing and dancing.

Discuss: Ask: **What were the people in the story happy about? What did they do? What did Jesus ride on?** Say: **Jesus is our King. We show He is our King by praising Him.**

6. The Snack Bin: Palm Leaf Picnic

Materials:: a sheet or tablecloth, animal crackers, juice, paper towels, wipes

Do: Spread a sheet or tablecloth across the floor and ask the children to sit on it. Say, **Some people waved their palm leaves when Jesus came by. Other people put their palm leaves on the ground to make a soft place for Jesus' donkey to walk on.** Encourage the children to put their palm leaves on the ground beside them. Ask them to clean their hands with the wipes. Pray, thanking God for Jesus and for the snack. Serve the animal crackers and juice.

Discuss: Ask children to tell you what kind of animal cracker they have and what sound that animal makes. Say, **Lions sing "roar." Horses sing "neigh." We sing "Tra-la-la! Hosanna to Jesus!" Jesus is our King. We show He is our King by praising Him.** Sing "Sing Hosanna" (page 31/track #74).

© Karyn Henley. All rights reserved.

Praise to God (CD Track #65)

Palm Leaf Pattern

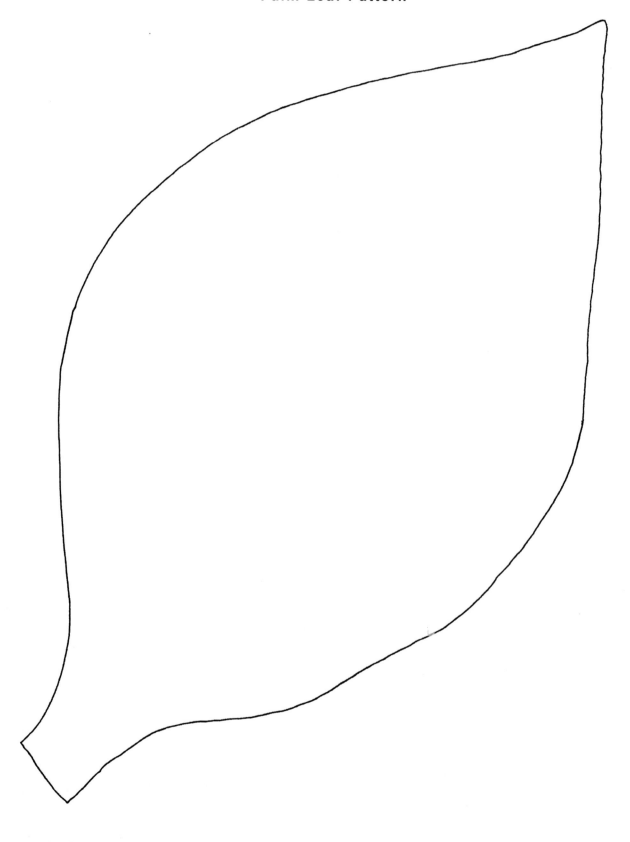

Playsongs Bible Time: Fours, Spring Quarter   37

Lesson 7

Easter: Jesus is Our Savior

Memory Verse for the Quarter: "Grow knowing Jesus." 2 Peter 3:18, ICB, simplified

Scripture "Praise to God in heaven!" Matthew 21:9, ICB

Bible Story The Resurrection, Matthew 28:1-8

Goal Learn that Jesus is our Savior: He died to save us from the power of sin. But God brought Him back to life.*

Today's Teacher Task
- Point out and describe sin, Jesus' death, and Jesus' resurrection.
- Repeat as often as appropriate:
  Jesus died to save us (make cross with one forefinger over the other)
  from the power of sin.
  Jesus is our Savior.
  God made Him alive again!* (arms up, outspread as if to cheer)

*Note: Death and life are abstract concepts for preschoolers. It's hard for young children to discern whether something is alive or not. So when we teach young children that Jesus died and came back to life, we know that they will not completely understand. However, we are laying a foundation for their future understanding.

INTRODUCTION

Materials: one cross shape cut from paper for each child (pattern on page 42), hole puncher, one 24-inch length of string or yarn for each child, uncooked hollow cylindrical pasta (ziti or rigatoni)

Do: As the children arrive, give each of them a length of string or yarn and a paper cross. Help them punch a hole in the top of the cross. They should thread the string through the hole, slide the cross to the center of the string and thread. Now they slide several tubes of pasta onto each side. Help them tie the string in the back to make a necklace, adjusting it to fit.

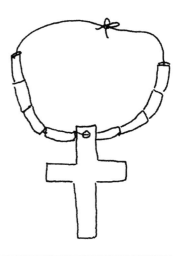

Discuss: Ask the children where they might see crosses in the world. (On church buildings, necklaces, key rings, the Red

© Karyn Henley. All rights reserved.

Cross, etc.) Ask them what the cross means. Say: **Easter is a time when we think about the cross, because Jesus died on a cross. Easter is also a time when we celebrate. What do we celebrate?**

LARGE GROUP TIME
Sing "Come to the Circle" (page 6/track #9), and gather the children together in a large group.

Bible Story

> **Materials:** a Bible with a marker at Matthew 27, a cross cut out of a large piece of construction paper or poster board, tape or a thumb tack or temporary plastic adhesive (like Plasti-Tak or Tak 'n Stik), a sheet, a pillow or large circle cut from poster board, a flashlight
>
> **Timesaver Option:** the <u>Before I Dream Bedtime Bible Storybook</u>

> **Do:** If you use the Bible storybook, read the story "Sadness and Joy."

If you don't use the storybook, tape or tack the cross to the wall or bulletin board within sight of the children. Drape the sheet over a table or chairs to make a small cave. Place a pillow or a big posterboard circle over the opening. Turn on a flashlight and turn off the classroom lights. Sit several feet away from the cross. Open the Bible to Matthew 27 and say, **Here's where the Bible tells about how Jesus died.** Shine the flashlight on the cross. **There were some men who didn't believe Jesus was God's Son. They got angry at Jesus and killed Him on a cross. God knew that would happen. Jesus knew that would happen. Jesus had never done anything wrong, but dying on the cross was the way He got in trouble for the bad things everybody else does. He got punished for you and me by dying on the cross.**

Turn the flashlight off. **When Jesus died, the day turned dark. Jesus' friends took his dead body and put it in a tomb.** Shine the flashlight on the sheet tomb. **They rolled a big stone over the opening to keep it closed. Early on Sunday morning, some of Jesus' friends went to the tomb. They were sad, because Jesus was dead, and they would miss Him.**

Now take the "stone" away from the tomb and ask the children to tiptoe over quietly and look inside to see if Jesus is there. Shine your flashlight in it so they can see. After everyone has looked, say, **Jesus was not in the tomb anymore. God had made Him come alive again! Hooray!** Ask the children to clap with you. Encourage them to all shout, **Jesus is alive!**

> **Discuss:** Teach the children the theme for the day:
> **Jesus died to save us** (make cross with one forefinger over the other)
> **from the power of sin.**
> **Jesus is our Savior.**
> **God made Him alive again!** (arms up, outspread as if to cheer)

© Karyn Henley. All rights reserved.

Songs and Movement

Sing "Growing Knowing Jesus" (page 6/track #28).
Sing the following song to the tune of "Mary Had a Little Lamb" (track #61).

On the day that Jesus died,	(fold hands and look sad)
People cried, people cried.	
On the day that Jesus died,	
They were very sad.	
Then when Jesus came alive,	(arms outspread; smile)
People smiled, people smiled.	
Then when Jesus came alive,	
They were very glad!	

Prayer

Ask the children to fold their hands and pray the words after you:
Dear God, Thank you for sending Jesus to die for our sins.
Thank you for bringing Him back to life again. Amen.

EXPLORE-A-BINS
Choose from these activities. Use them in the order that best suits your needs.

1. The Art Bin: Sponge–Painted Crosses

Materials: newspaper or a plastic tablecloth, rectangular sponges cut into cross shapes, light blue construction paper, one or more paper plates, brown washable preschool paint, paper towels, hand wipes

Do: Give each child a cross-shaped sponge and a piece of paper. Cover the bottom of one or more paper plates with paint. Show children how to press the sponge into the paint and then onto the paper to make cross prints.

Discuss: As the children work, ask: **Where do you see crosses? What happened on the cross? Did Jesus stay dead? What happened? Where is Jesus now?** Say: **Jesus died to save us from the power of sin. Jesus is our Savior. God made Him alive again!** Sing "On the Day that Jesus Died" (above).

2. The Science-Math Bin: Who Is It?

Materials: none

Do: Tell the children what you will be doing in this activity. Then seat the children in a circle. Ask one child to be the Guesser. He close his eyes. Point to another child. That child quietly moves into the center of the circle. Then that child says, "Jesus is alive!" The Guesser must guess who was talking. Then the Guesser gets to choose the next Guesser.

© Karyn Henley. All rights reserved.

Discuss: Stop the game in time to discuss it: **How do you know who was talking? God has made our ears to hear many sounds. He has made our minds to think about how the sounds are different. What sad sound do you think you would have heard from Jesus' friends after Jesus died?** (crying) **What happy sound did Jesus' friends make after they found out Jesus was not dead anymore?** (Jesus is alive! Praise God! Hooray!) Say: **Jesus died to save us from the power of sin. Jesus is our Savior. God made Him alive again!** Sing "On the Day that Jesus Died" (page 39/track #61).

3. **The Look and Listen Bin: Jesus is Alive!**

    Materials: books and/or CDs/DVDs about Palm Sunday, Easter, praise and singing, CD/DVD player

    You may use your own books and CDs/DVDs. The following are suggestions:
    <u>Mary and the Empty Tomb</u> by Alice Joyce Davidson
    <u>He is Alive</u> by Helen Haidle   <u>The Easter Story</u> by Brian Wildsmith
    <u>Hurry, Hurry!</u> by Mary Manz Simon   <u>Easter ABC's</u> by Isabel Anders
    <u>J is for Jesus</u> by Debbie Trafton O'Neal   <u>The Story of Easter</u> by Aileen Fisher
    <u>My First Hymnal</u>, CD by Karyn Henley
    <u>Before I Dream Bedtime Bible Storybook</u>, "Sadness and Joy" by Karyn Henley
    "L-O-V-E" from <u>PlaySongs: Five Little Ladybugs</u> CD/DVD by Karyn Henley
    <u>L-O-V-E</u>, a PlaySongs book about Jesus' death and resurrection by Karyn Henley
    "Praise Him, Praise Him" from <u>PlaySongs: Tiny Treasures</u> CD/DVD by Karyn Henley

    Do: Read the book(s) or let the children look at the pictures while you point out anything that has to do with Easter or praising God. Play any CDs or DVDs that you've chosen.

    Discuss: Say: **Jesus died to save us from the power of sin. Jesus is our Savior. God made Him alive again!** Sing "On the Day that Jesus Died" (page 39/track #61).

4. **The Creative Movement Bin: Jesus is Alive!**

    Materials: none

    Do: Encourage the children to copy you as you lead them in the following action songs or rhymes.

    <u>Everyone Is Glad!</u> (track #16)

Jesus' body was put in a tomb	(hands cupped together)
And everyone was sad.	(make a sad face)
But God made Him alive!	
Now there's no one inside	(peek inside cupped hands)
And everyone is glad.	(hold hands out and smile)

<u>If You're Happy and You Know It</u> (traditional tune/track #43)

If you're happy and you know it, clap your hands*.	(clap, clap)
If you're happy and you know it, clap your hands.	(clap, clap)
If you're happy and you know it,	
Then your face will surely show it.	(smile)
If you're happy and you know it, clap your hands.	(clap, clap)

*For other verses, tap your feet, nod your head, touch your nose, etc.

Discuss: Say: **Jesus died to save us from the power of sin. Jesus is our Savior. God made Him alive again!**

5. The Game Bin: Jesus Is Alive!

Materials: none

Do: Divide the children into two groups, Group 1 and Group 2. Tell the children to crouch down. Tell them that when you clap once, Group 1 should jump up and say, "Jesus is alive!" When you clap two times, Group 2 should jump up and say, "Jesus is alive!" When you clap three times, both groups should jump up and say, "Jesus is alive!" Now say, **When Jesus died on the cross, his friends were sad. They put his body in a tomb. But on Sunday morning, they went to the tomb. They looked inside, but it was empty.** Now clap once or twice or three times. Then ask a child to tell the story and choose the number of times to clap. Continue, asking different children to tell the story each time. Stop the game in time to have a brief discussion.

Discuss: Ask: **What happened on the cross? Did Jesus stay dead? What happened? Where is Jesus now?** Say: **Jesus died to save us from the power of sin. Jesus is our Savior. God made Him alive again!** Sing "On the Day that Jesus Died" (page 39/track #61).

6. The Snack Bin: Happy Face Snacks

Materials: bread or sliced biscuits, jelly in a squirt bottle, juice, paper plates and cups, paper towels, hand wipes

Do: Help the children wash their hands with wipes. Pray, thanking God for Jesus and for the snack. Give each child a piece of bread or half of a biscuit. Squirt jelly onto the bread or biscuit, making a happy face (a smile and two eyes).
Discuss: As the children eat, ask: **Why were Jesus' friends sad when he died? What made them happy again?** Say: **Jesus died to save us from the power of sin. Jesus is our Savior. God made Him alive again!** Sing "On the Day that Jesus Died" (page 39/track #61).

© Karyn Henley. All rights reserved.

Cross Necklace Pattern

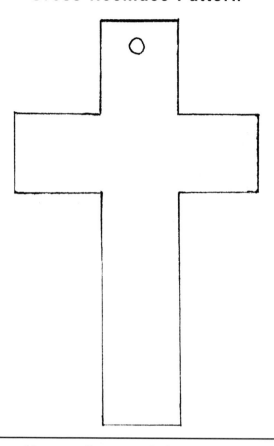

Nurse Cap and Arm Band

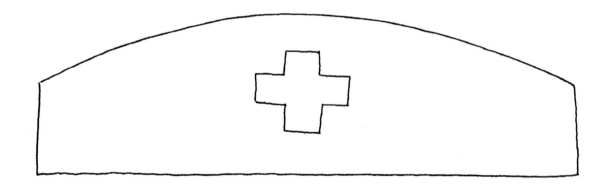

© Karyn Henley. All rights reserved.

Playsongs Bible Time: Fours, Spring Quarter

Lesson 8

Jesus is a Healer

Memory Verse for the Quarter: "Grow knowing Jesus." 2 Peter 3:18, ICB, simplified

Scripture   "Jesus healed many who had different kinds of sicknesses."
Mark 1:34, ICB

Bible Story   Jesus heals a man's bent hand, Luke 6:6–11

Goal   Learn that Jesus has the power to make us well.

Today's Teacher Task
- Point out things that indicate sickness and wellness.
- Repeat as often as appropriate:
  Jesus healed a man's bent hand.   (right hand in a fist; stretch it out)
  Jesus can make us well.   (left hand in a fist; stretch it out)

INTRODUCTION

Materials: hand towels or bath towels or pillowcases or baby blankets, stuffed animals, toy doctors' kits

Do: As the children arrive, show them how to hold the towels, pillowcases or blankets between them, one child on each end. Put a stuffed animal on the towel and encourage the children to carry the animal on this "stretcher" to the doctor (across the room). Ask some of the children to be the doctors and nurses for the sick animals. They can use the equipment in the doctors' kits. Encourage children to take turns, some being doctors and nurses, others being rescue workers.

Option: Each child holds a towel, pulling it behind him with the animal on it.

Discuss: Ask: **Did you ever get sick? How does it feel? Who takes you to the doctor? How do doctors and nurses help?**

LARGE GROUP TIME
Sing "Come to the Circle" (page 6/track #9), and gather the children together in a large group.

Bible Story

Materials: a Bible with a bookmark at Luke 6

In class, open the Bible to Luke 6 and say: **Here's where the Bible tells about a man who had a bent hand.** Ask the children to curl their hands into a fist as if their hands are bent and can't straighten out. **Could you draw with that hand? Could you hold a spoon or fork? Could you wash your face or brush your teeth? One day this man was at the worship house. Jesus saw him there. Jesus told the man to stand up.** Ask the children to stand up with one hand still in a fist. **Jesus asked the other people, "Should we hurt people or help them?"** Ask the children how they would answer that question. **Jesus said to the man, "Let me see your hand." The man stretched his hand out all the way.** Ask the children to straighten their hands back out. **The man was well! Thank you, Jesus! Jesus healed the man's bent hand! Jesus can make us well.**

Songs and Movement

Sing "Growing Knowing Jesus" (page 6/track #28).
Sing "Jesus Made the Sick Man Well" to the tune of "Mary Had a Little Lamb."
   On the words *sick man*, hold your hands in a fist.
   On the words *well*, open your hand:

> **Jesus made the sick man well,**
> **Sick man well, sick man well.**
> **Jesus made the sick man well.**
> **Thank you, thank you, God.**

Prayer

Ask the children to fold their hands and pray the words after you:
   Dear God, Thank you that Jesus has the power to make people well. Amen.

EXPLORE-A-BINS™
Choose from these activities. Use them in the order that best suits your needs.

1. The Art Bin: Nurse Cap and Arm Band

Materials: a cap front and arm band for each child copied and cut out from page 42, red crayons, a 1-inch x 20-inch strip of construction paper or posterboard for each child, a stapler and staples, tape

Do: Give each child a cap front and arm band. Ask the children to color the cross red. Then staple or tape each cap front to the center of a paper strip. Curve the strip around to fit the child's head. Staple or tape it in place. Fit the arm band to the child's arm. Tape it in place.

Discuss: As the children work, ask: **Have you ever heard of the Red Cross? People who work at the Red Cross take care of people who are hurt or sick. When you**

get sick, who takes care of you? What does a doctor do? What does a nurse do? Who was sick in our story? What happened? Why do we pray for people who are sick? Say: Jesus healed the man's bent hand! Jesus can make us well.** Sing "Jesus Made the Sick Man Well" (above).

2. **The Science-Math Bin: Doctors and Dolls**

   Materials: toy doctor kits, a real stethoscope if possible, adhesive strip bandages of different sizes, baby dolls, pillows and blankets, baby beds or boxes

   Do: Encourage the children to pretend that the baby dolls are sick. They can take care of the dolls by putting them in the beds, putting bandages on them, etc. The children may also put bandages on themselves and cover themselves up with blankets. Let them listen to their own hearts with the stethoscope.

   Discuss: Talk about feeling well and feeling sick. Ask: **Why would someone need a bandage? How do doctors and nurses help? How did Jesus help the man with the bent hand?** Say: **Jesus healed the man's bent hand! Jesus can make us well.** Sing "Jesus Made the Sick Man Well" (page 44).

3. **The Look and Listen Bin: When I'm Sick**

   Materials: books and/or CDs/DVDs about being sick or about Jesus, CD/DVD player

   You may use your own books and CDs/DVDs. The following are suggestions:
   "A Sick Boy" and "Jesus Made the Sick Boy Well" from My Thank You Bible
      Stories & Songs CD by Karyn Henley
   Jesus Loves the Little Children, Jesus is With Me, or Jesus Loves Me by
      Debby Anderson
   Doctor Maisy by Lucy Cousins
   Bear Feels Sick by Karma Wilson
   Story "Hezekiah Gets Well" and Song "When I'm Sick in Bed" from My Learn to Pray
      Bible by Karyn Henley
   "God Will Never Stop Loving Me," on PlaySongs: Grow, Grow, Grow CD/DVD by
      Karyn Henley

   Do: Read the book(s) or let the children look at the book(s) while you point out the things that have to do with being sick, or with Jesus' love and care. Play any CDs/DVDs you've chosen.

   Discuss: Talk about how God loves us even when we're sick. Ask: **How did Jesus help the man with the bent hand?** Say: **Jesus healed the man's bent hand! Jesus can make us well.** Sing "Jesus Made the Sick Man Well" (page 44).

4. The Creative Movement Bin: Getting Well

Materials: none

 Do: Encourage the children to copy you as you do the following action songs.

The Doctor   (to the tune of "Old McDonald Had a Farm"/track #78)

The doctor listens to my heart, **Thump-a-thump-a-thump.** **And he hears every little part,** **Thump-a-thump-a-thump.** **There's a thump-thump here** **And a thump-thump there,** **Here a thump, there a thump,** **Everywhere a thump-thump.** **The doctor listens to my heart,** **Thump-a-thump-a-thump.**	(On this verse, pat your chest. Gently pat the children's chests.)

For other verses, sing:

The doctor says to open wide, **Ahh-ahh-ahh.** **And he looks way down deep inside,** **Ahh-ahh-ahh. . . .**	(Encourage the children to open wide and say "Ahh" on this verse.)
The doctor looks into my ears, **Shh-shh-shh.** **He wants to know how well I hear.** **Shh-shh-shh. . . .**	(Hold hands behind ears.) (Fingers to lips.) (Hands behind ears.) (Fingers to lips.)

Going to the Doctor   (to the tune of "Go In and Out the Window"/track #27)
Ask the children to pretend their elbows are hurt. Each child puts one hand on his own elbow as he marches around the circle and sings:

I'm going to the doctor,
I'm going to the doctor,
I'm going to the doctor,
Lord Jesus, make me well!

The children can suggest different parts of their bodies that are hurt: knee, shoulder, chin, etc. Each child must put a hand on that place as he marches (or hops or skips or tiptoes) around, singing the verse.

Discuss: Say: **Jesus healed the man's bent hand! Jesus can make us well.**

© Karyn Henley. All rights reserved.

5. **The Game Bin: Hide the Medicine Bottle**

    Materials: a clean, empty plastic medicine bottle

    Do: Hide the medicine bottle in a place where children can find it. Then ask them to look for it. Tell them when they are close and when they are far away from it. The child who finds the medicine bottle gets to hide it while the other children close their eyes.

    Discuss: Ask: **How does medicine help us get well? How does praying help us get well? Did the person in our story take medicine to get well? What happened?** Say: **Jesus healed the man's bent hand! Jesus can make us well.** Sing "Jesus Made the Sick Man Well" (page 44).

6. **The Snack Bin: Healthy Foods**

    Materials: blueberries, vanilla yogurt, plastic spoons, paper bowls, paper towels, hand wipes

    Do: Ask the children to clean their hands with wipes. Pray, thanking Jesus for taking care of us when we're sick. Thank God for the snack. Give each child a bowl. Spoon some yogurt into each bowl. Ask the children to drop a few berries on top of their yogurt. Give each child a spoon. Ask the children to stir the berries into the yogurt, then eat the snack.

    Discuss: Talk about good foods that God gave us to help keep us well. Ask: **How do doctors and nurses help? How did Jesus help the man with the bent hand?** Say: **Jesus healed the man's bent hand! Jesus can make us well.** Sing "Jesus Made the Sick Man Well" (page 44).

Lesson 9

Jesus is Worthy of Praise

Memory Verse for the Quarter: "Grow knowing Jesus." 2 Peter 3:18, ICB, simplified

Scripture   "All the people praised him (Jesus)." Luke 4:15

Bible Story   Jesus heals a bent–over woman, Luke 13:10–13

Goal   Learn that Jesus is worthy of praise. That means Jesus is so wonderful, we can always say, "You're the best, Jesus!"

Today's Teacher Task
- Point out things things we can praise Jesus for.
- Repeat as often as appropriate:
  Jesus is so wonderful, we praise Him!   (arms outspread)
  You're the best, Jesus!   (clap)

INTRODUCTION

Materials: one bendable drinking straw for each child, scissors for teacher, long chenille wire (pipe cleaners), play dough*

Note: You can use store-bought play dough, or make it yourself, or let the children make it as part of the activity. To make play dough, mix 1 part water, 1 part salt, and 3 parts flour.

Do: Before class, cut about 1/2-inch slit through both sides of the end of the straw closest to the bend. As children arrive, help them fold the chenille wire in half. Then they twist the wires together about halfway down the fold and open up the bend, forming a circle, which is the head of the figure. Pull the ends of the wire so they are sticking out like arms. Help the children slip the twist of the wire into

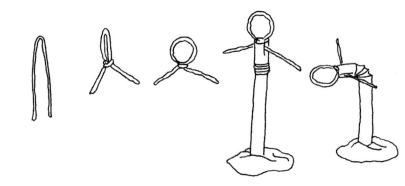

the straw at the slit as shown. Now give each child a handful of play dough to make a mound into which to stick the bottom end of the straw. Then show the children how to bend their figures by bending the straw. These will become the story figures.

Discuss: Ask: **Why do we bend over?** (to pick things up, to sit down, to exercise, to look between your legs to see behind you, to put on your shoes and socks, to catch a rolling ball, etc.) **What if you bent over and couldn't stand back up? Our story today is about someone who couldn't stand up straight.**

LARGE GROUP TIME
Sing "Come to the Circle" (page 6/track #9), and gather the children together in a large group.

Bible Story

  Materials: a Bible with a bookmark at Luke 13, the figures the children made in the introductory activity

  Note: If you didn't do the introductory activity, you may make one figure for yourself before class to help you tell the story, or you may make one for each child and hand them out before the story so the children can help tell the story.

  Do: In class, open the Bible to Luke 13 and say: **Here's where the Bible tells about a woman who was bent over. She couldn't stand up straight.** Bend your figure over. If the children have figures, ask them to bend their figures over as well. **Jesus was teaching lots of people about God. When he looked around at the people, He saw a woman who had been bent over for 18 years! Jesus called her to come over to Him. He put his hand on her and said, "Your sickness is gone." Right away she could stand up straight and tall.** Straighten your figure and/or ask the children to straighten theirs. **She praised God.**

  Discuss: Say: **The woman praised God, because Jesus made her well. What else can we praise Jesus for? Jesus is so wonderful, we praise Him! You're the best, Jesus!** Lead the children to clap for Jesus.

Songs and Movement
  Sing "Growing Knowing Jesus" (page 6/track #28).
  Sing "Jesus Made the Bent Woman Well" to the tune of "Mary Had a Little Lamb" (track #51). Ask the children to stand. On the words *bent woman*, everyone bends over. On the word *well*, stand straight:

  **Jesus made the bent woman well, bent woman well, bent woman well.
  Jesus made the bent woman well. Thank you, thank you, God.**

© Karyn Henley. All rights reserved.

Prayer
Ask the children to fold their hands and pray the words after you:
Dear God, Thank you that Jesus has the power to make people well. We praise you, Jesus! You're the best! Amen.

EXPLORE-A-BINS
Choose from these activities. Use them in the order that best suits your needs.

1. The Art Bin: Paper Tube Figures

Materials: a 4 1/2-inch long cardboard tube for each child from a roll of toilet paper or paper towels or gift wrap, markers, yarn or cotton balls or fringed construction paper, glue, small adhesive bandages

Note: You can make tubes by rolling paper into a cylinder and stapling or taping it.

Do: Give each child a cardboard tube. Ask the children to draw facial features on their tubes with a marker. Ask them to glue yarn, cotton balls or fringed construction paper on top to make hair. Then ask them to put a small adhesive bandage on this figure.

Discuss: As the children work, ask: **Did you ever get sick? What happened? Why do we pray for people who are sick? Who was sick in our story? What happened? What did the bent woman do when she found out she was well?** She praised God. **What else can people praise Jesus for?** Say: **Jesus is so wonderful, we praise Him! You're the best, Jesus!** Sing "Jesus Made the Bent Woman Well" (page 49/track #51).

2. The Science-Math Bin: Wrapping the Hurt Place

Materials: strips of gauze bandages, other kinds of bandages

Do: Ask the children to compare the different types of bandages. Let children loosely wrap the gauze bandages around parts of their bodies (but not their necks). Talk about the names of the parts that they wrap: elbows, ankles, wrists, knees, shoulders, etc. Ask what the function of that body part is and what kinds of things would be hard to do if that part was hurt.

Discuss: As the children work, ask: **What's a cast? Did you ever have to wear a cast or know someone who wore one? Why would the doctor wrap up a hurt place? What was wrong with the sick person in our story? What happened? Why do we pray for sick people? What did the bent woman do when she found out she was well? She praised God. What else can people praise Jesus for?** Say: **Jesus is so wonderful, we praise Him! You're the best, Jesus!** Sing "Jesus Made the Bent Woman Well" (page 49/track #51).

3. **The Look and Listen Bin: When I'm Sick**

    Materials: books and/or CDs/DVDs about being sick or about praising Jesus, CD/DVD player

    You may use your own books and CDs/DVDs. The following are suggestions:
      "A Sick Boy" and "Jesus Made the Sick Boy Well" from My Thank You
        Bible Stories and Songs CD by Karyn Henley
    Jesus Loves Me, Jesus Loves the Little Children, or Jesus is With Me by
        Debby Anderson
    Doctor Maisy by Lucy Cousins
    Bear Feels Sick by Karma Wilson
    My First Hymnal, CD by Karyn Henley
    Give Thanks to the Lord or Let's Make a Joyful Noise by Karma Wilson
    Story "Hezekiah Gets Well" and Song "When I'm Sick In Bed" from My Learn to Pray
        Bible by Karyn Henley
    Any of the following from Playsongs CDs/DVDs by Karyn Henley:
      "Kitchen Band Parade," "Kitchen Band Chant," "Thank You, God, for Me," "I Like to
        Play Music," from Noah's Zoo
      "Happy Kids" and "Praise the Lord" from I Feel Like a Giggle
      "Great Big God" from Grow, Grow, Grow
      "It's a Beautiful World" and "I Really Wanta' Tell Ya" from Down by the Station
      "Tiny Treasures" and "Praise Him, Praise Him" from Tiny Treausres

Do: Read the book(s) or let the children look at the book(s) while you point out the things that have to do with being sick, or with praising God and Jesus. Play any CDs/DVDs you've chosen.

Discuss: Ask: **What did the bent woman do when she found out she was well? She praised God.** Say: **Jesus is so wonderful, we praise Him! You're the best, Jesus!**

© Karyn Henley. All rights reserved.

4. The Creative Movement Bin: Praise Songs

Materials: rhythm instruments or paper cups with the bottoms punched out, CDs/DVDs to sing and play along with, CD/DVD player

CD/DVD Suggestions:
"I Like to Play Music," from PlaySongs: Noah's Zoo by Karyn Henley
"Psalm 150," from PlaySongs: Five Little Ladybugs by Karyn Henley
"Rock-a-My Soul" and "Thank You March" from PlaySongs: I Feel Like a Giggle by Karyn Henley

Do: Encourage the children to play their instruments as you sing together or play the songs from the CDs/DVDs.

If you prefer not to use recorded music, you can sing the following song as the children march, clap, and sing or blow through the paper cups.

Joyful Noise   (to the tune of "Oh Where Have You Been, Billy Boy?"/track #56)
   Oh, make a joyful noise to the Lord, all the earth,
   Oh, make a joyful noise to the Lord.
   Oh, make a joyful noise
   All you girls and all you boys,
   Oh, come make a joyful, joyful noise.

Discuss: Ask: **What did the bent woman do when she found out she was well? She praised God. What else can we praise Jesus for?** Say: **Jesus is so wonderful, we praise Him! You're the best, Jesus!**

5. The Game Bin: Doctor, Doctor, Where Am I Sick?

Materials: none

Do: Ask children to stand on one side of the room. Choose one child to be the "doctor" standing on the opposite side of the room facing the others. The children chant, "Doctor, doctor, where am I sick?" The doctor says, "Head" or "Tummy" or "Arm," etc. The children must hold that place while they jump across the room to the doctor. Then the doctor chooses a child to take his place at the opposite side of the room, and play continues. Stop the game in time for a brief discussion.

Discuss: Ask: **How do doctors help when we are sick? How does God help? Who was sick in our story? What happened? What did the bent woman do when she found out she was well? She praised God. What else can we praise Jesus for?** Say: **Jesus is so wonderful, we praise Him! You're the best, Jesus!**

6. The Snack Bin: Red Cross Buns

Materials: English muffins, whipped cream cheese, tubes of ready made red frosting or red jelly in a squirt bottle, juice, paper plates and cups, plastic picnic spoons, paper towels, hand wipes

Do: Ask the children to clean their hands with wipes. Pray, praising Jesus for the wonderful things he's done. Thank God for the snack. Give each child a paper plate, a spoon, and one half of an English muffin. Spoon some cream cheese on top of each muffin and ask the children to spread it around with the back of their spoons. Help the children squirt red frosting or jelly on top of the cream cheese in the shape of a cross.

Discuss: As you help children prepare the snack, ask: **Have you ever seen something with a big red cross on it? What does the red cross mean? Who was sick in our story? What happened? What did the bent woman do when she found out she was well? She praised God. What else can we praise Jesus for?** Say: **Jesus is so wonderful, we praise Him! You're the best, Jesus!** Sing "Jesus Made the Bent Woman Well" (page 49/track #51).

54 Playsongs Bible Time: Fours, Spring Quarter

Lesson 10

Jesus Cares About Us

Memory Verse for the Quarter: "Grow knowing Jesus." 2 Peter 3:18, ICB, simplified

Scripture "Give all your worries to him, because he cares for you." 1 Peter 5:7

Bible Story Jesus walks on water, Matthew 14:22-33

Goal Learn that Jesus cares about our feelings.

Today's Teacher Task
- Point out feelings.
- Repeat as often as appropriate:
    Jesus cared that his friends were scared.
    Jesus cares how we feel, and He helps us.

INTRODUCTION

Materials: paper plates, scissors for teacher, tape, crayons

Do: Cut paper plates in half. Let the children color the plates. Then show them how to hold the center of the straight edge and wave the half-plates like fans, creating "wind." If your room has windows and there is a breeze or wind outdoors, ask the children to look out and tell you how they know the wind is blowing.

Discuss: Ask: **Does the wind blow where you live? What moves when the wind blows?** (clouds, trees, flags, our hair, etc.) **What does not move when the wind blows?** (rocks, buildings - unless it's a tornado wind or hurricane wind) **Who takes care of you when the wind blows?**

LARGE GROUP TIME
Sing "Come to the Circle" (page 6/track #9), and gather the children together in a large group.

Bible Story

Materials: a Bible with a bookmark at Matthew 14, a blue bedsheet or tablecloth

Do: In class, open the Bible to Matthew 4 and say: **Here's where the Bible tells about a time when Jesus was praying up in the mountains. He had told his**

© Karyn Henley. All rights reserved.

friends to go ahead and sail across the lake in their boat. Spread the sheet out on the floor and ask the children to sit around it. Ask two children to get in the middle of the sheet and pretend to sail. **But the wind was blowing against them.** Ask the rest of the children to hold the edge of the sheet and shake it to ripple the "water." **They tried to sail, but they couldn't get anywhere. Late in the night, Jesus came to them, walking on the water. They were scared. They thought they were seeing a ghost.** Ask all the children to show what a scared face might look like. **But Jesus said, "Don't be scared. It's me." Peter said, "If it's you, let me walk to you on the water." Jesus said, "Come on."** Ask one of the children on the sheet to stand and step across the sheet while the others keep making waves. **Peter walked out on the water. But then he saw the waves, and he got scared. He started to sink.** Ask the children holding the edges of the sheet to slowly raise the sheet edges higher and higher so the child in the middle appears to be sinking. **Peter called, "Help, Jesus!" Then Jesus reached out pulled Peter out of the water.** Ask the children to lower the sheet. **Jesus walked back to the boat with Peter. They both got in, and the wind stopped blowing.** Ask the children to let go of the edge of the sheet.

Discuss: Ask: **When have you been scared? Did Jesus care? What other kinds of feelings do you have?** (happy, sad, bored, angry, worried) **Does Jesus care about your feelings?** Say: **Jesus cared that his friends were scared. Jesus cares how we feel, and He helps us.**

Songs and Movement

Sing the memory verse song, "Growing Knowing Jesus" (page 6/track #28).
Sing "Jesus Cares" to the tune of "Mary Had a Little Lamb":

**Jesus cares when I am scared*,
I am scared, I am scared.
Jesus cares when I am scared,
Jesus is my friend.**

*For more verses, substitute other feelings: happy, sad, bored, angry, worried, etc.)

Prayer

Ask the children to fold their hands and pray the words after you:
Dear God, Thank you that Jesus cares how we feel. Amen.

EXPLORE-A-BINS
Choose from these activities. Use them in the order that best suits your needs.

1. The Art Bin: Making Waves

Materials: blue play dough*, paper plates, paper towels, optional: boat stickers

*Note: If you want to make a soft play dough, mix 1 cup of vegetable oil, 6 cups of flour, and 1 cup of water. Add blue food coloring.

Do: Give each child a paper plate and some blue play dough to represent a lake. Ask the children to make waves on top of the plate with the dough. Give each child a boat sticker to stick into his lake.

Discuss: As the children work, ask: **What are waves? What is wind? What kind of weather came while Jesus and his friends were in their boat? How did Jesus' friends feel? Did Jesus care? What did Jesus do?** Say: **Jesus cared that his friends were scared. Jesus cares how we feel, and He helps us.** Sing "Jesus Cares" (page 55).

2. The Science-Math Bin: Surface Tension

Materials: a coffee cup, water, pennies, a bath towel, paper towels

Do: Lay the bath towel across a table. Place the coffee cup in the center. Pour water into the cup until it's almost up to the rim of the cup. Ask the children to lower themselves until their eyes are right in line with the cup. Ask them to watch the rim of the cup as they count the pennies you slip into the water. Slowly slip one coin in. Then another. After a few coins, they should see the water level barely rising above the rim of the cup. Ask what keeps the water from pouring out. It's something called "surface tension." It's almost like a thin skin on top of the water. But when it's stretched too tightly, it breaks. Ask the children if they think the next coin will break it. Slip in another coin. If the water doesn't spill, ask if the next coin will break it. Keep going until the water spills out.

Discuss: Ask: **How could Jesus walk on water?** (He is God's Son. He has all power. The water has to hold Him up if He tells it to.) **How did Jesus' friends feel when they saw Him coming toward them on the water? Did Jesus care? What did Peter do? Why did Peter sink? Did Jesus care? When might you get scared? Does Jesus care?** Say: **Jesus cared that his friends were scared. Jesus cares how we feel, and He helps us.** Sing "Jesus Cares" (page 55).

3. The Look and Listen Bin: Jesus Cares How We Feel

Materials: books and/or CDs/DVDs about boats or lakes or Jesus' love and care, CD/DVD player

You may choose your own books and CDs/DVDs. Some suggestions are:
  Jesus Loves Me, Jesus Loves the Little Children, or Jesus is With Me
    by Debby Anderson
"I Am Your God," from PlaySongs: Noah's Zoo CD/DVD by Karyn Henley
Boats by Byron Barton   Nicole's Boat by Allen Morgan
Busy Boats by Tony Mitton & Ant Parker   Mr. Gumpy's Outing by John Burningham
Story "Paul Says Thanks" and Song "I Pray, 'Thank You'" from My Learn To Pray
    Bible by Karyn Henley

Do: Read the book(s) or let the children look at the book(s) while you point out the things that have to do with wind and waves, or with feelings, or with Jesus' love and care. Play any CDs/DVDs you've chosen.

Discuss: Ask: **When might you get scared? When might you be happy? When might you be sad? Does Jesus care how you feel?** Say: **Jesus cared that his friends were scared. Jesus cares how we feel, and He helps us.** Sing "Jesus Cares" (page 55).

4. The Creative Movement Bin: Waves, Be Still

Materials: a 1' x 2' strip of blue sheer fabric or scarf for each child, or a blue streamer for each child

Do: Encourage the children to copy you as you do the following action plays.

Waves, Waves, Splash Away   (to the tune of "Rain, Rain, Go Away")

Waves, waves, splash away	(clap gently and quickly)
On this windy, windy day.	

Repeat the above verse two more times, the first time patting your legs and the second time marching.

Flash Goes the Lightning   (to the tune of "Pop Goes the Weasel"/track #18)

It's a rainy, rainy day,	(squat; pat hands on floor)
The raindrops are falling.	
Splashing down around the town,	
Flash! goes the lightning.	(pop up)
It's a rainy, rainy day,	(squat; pat hands on floor)
The thunder is rumbling,	
Rumbling all around the town,	
Flash! goes the lightning.	(pop up)

Wavy Water   (track #91)
Give each child a strip of fabric or a streamer. Show them how to pretend to be wavy water by holding the fabric, lifting it up, and bringing it down again.

Wavy water, wave so slowly	(Stand and wave fabric slowly.)
Wavy water, wave so fast.	(Wave the fabric quickly.)
Wavy water, up and down.	
Wavy water, splash!	(Jump and then squat.)

Discuss: Say: **Jesus cared that his friends were scared. How did He help them? Jesus cares how we feel, and He helps us.** Sing "Jesus Cares" (page 55).

© Karyn Henley. All rights reserved.

5. The Game Bin: Storm Freeze

Materials: none

Do: When you say "storm," the children move around the room as if they are being blown by a storm. When you say "freeze," the children stop and stand still in whatever position they find themselves. Choose a child to call the words for the next round. Then that child chooses another child to call the words. Try to give everyone a chance to call "storm" or "freeze." Stop in time to have a brief discussion.

Discuss: Ask the children to tell about any storms they have seen. Ask: **How did you feel in the storm? Did Jesus care?** Say: **Jesus cared that his friends were scared. How did He help them? Jesus cares how we feel, and He helps us.** Sing "Jesus Cares" (page 55).

6. The Snack Bin: Wave Muffins

Materials: sliced English muffins, whipped cream cheese with blue food coloring mixed in it, juice, plastic spoons, paper plates and cups, paper towels, hand wipes

Do: Ask the children to wash their hands with wipes. Pray, thanking God that Jesus cares about how we feel. Give each child a paper plate and half of an English muffin. Spread each muffin half with blue cream cheese. Give the children plastic spoons, and show them how to use the spoons to make wave-like peaks in the cream cheese.

Discuss: Ask the children to tell about any storms they have seen. Ask: **How did you feel in the storm? Did Jesus care?** Say: **Jesus cared that his friends were scared. How did He help them? Jesus cares how we feel, and He helps us.** Sing "Jesus Cares" (page 55). Ask the children to describe other feelings they have.

Lesson 11

Jesus Loves All People

Memory Verse for the Quarter: "Grow knowing Jesus." 2 Peter 3:18, ICB, simplified

Scripture Jesus said, "Love each other as I have loved you." John 15:12, NIV

Bible Story The woman at the well, John 4:1-42

Goal Learn that Jesus loves all people everywhere.

Today's Teacher Task
- Point out signs of Jesus' love (what He's given us, what He's done for us).
- Repeat as often as appropriate:
    Jesus loves all people.
    He wants us to love all people too.

INTRODUCTION

Materials: heart shapes cut from different patterns of gift wrap (two hearts from each kind of wrap - heart sample shapes are on page 64)

Option: Instead of gift wrap, you can cut hearts from different colors of construction paper, two hearts of each color.

Do: As children arrive, ask them to form a circle and put their hands behind their backs. Walk around the circle, placing a heart in each child's hands. When you say go, they look at their hearts and quickly try to find the child who has the matching pattern or color of heart. When they've found that child, they sit down together where they are. When all are seated, take up the hearts, shuffle them and play the game again, including any children who arrived while the first round of play was going on.

Discuss: Ask: **What does a heart make us think about? How do we know if someone loves us? How can we show our love for others?**

LARGE GROUP TIME
Sing "Come to the Circle" (page 6/track #9), and gather the children together in a large group.

Bible Story

Materials: a Bible with a bookmark at John 4, boxes or blocks, a real pitcher of water, paper cups

Do: Make a well by stacking boxes or blocks on top of each other in a circle, or by making a small circle of chairs. Place the pitcher of water in the well. Now gently hold the Bible and say, **Here's where the Bible tells about a woman from a different country.** Encourage the children to follow you as you walk around the room. Say: **When Jesus traveled, He didn't go in a car or airplane or train. He walked. Sometimes He walked a long, long way. He got very tired. One day, Jesus was traveling a different country called Samaria. People from Jesus' country didn't like the people from Samaria. But Jesus saw a well in Samaria, a deep place in the ground where there was water.** Point to the well. **He was tired, so He sat down by the well to rest.** Encourage the children to sit with you by the well. **Soon, a lady from Samaria came to the well to get water. Jesus asked her for a drink. The lady was surprised that Jesus would even talk to her, because she knew people from Jesus' country would not like her. But Jesus talked to her, and she gave Him some water.** Get the pitcher out of the well pour a cup of water for each child. **She went back to town and called all her friends to come and meet Jesus. Jesus talked with them, too. They asked Jesus to stay in their town for awhile, and He stayed for two days.**

Discuss: Ask if anyone knows someone from a different country. **Sometimes people have a hard time liking other people from other countries, or people who are different. But Jesus loves all people. He wants us to love all people too.**

Songs and Movement

Sing the memory verse song, "Growing Knowing Jesus" (page 6/track #28).
Sing "Jesus Loves Us Everyone" to the tune of "London Bridge" (track #50):

**Jesus loves us everyone, everyone, everyone,
Jesus loves us everyone. Thank you, Jesus.**

**Jesus loves us tall or small, tall or small, tall or small,
Jesus loves us tall or small. Thank you, Jesus.**

**Jesus loves us dark or light, dark or light, dark or light,
Jesus loves us dark or light. Thank you, Jesus.**

Prayer

Ask the children to fold their hands and pray the words after you:
Dear God, Thank you that Jesus loves all people. Help us love all people too.
                        Amen.

EXPLORE-A-BINS
Choose from these activities. Use them in the order that best suits your needs.

1. The Art Bin: Profiles

Materials: one large piece of manila paper for each child, crayons

Do: Give each child a piece of manila paper. Ask the child to lay the side of his head down on one end of the paper with his nose pointing to the center. Draw around his profile. Let the child choose a friend who will lay his head on the other side of the paper, with his nose pointing to the center. Draw around this child's profile too. Help the children write their names under their profiles. Then they can color them.

Discuss: As the children work, ask them to tell how they are like the friend they chose. Ask how they are different from that friend. Ask: **How did Jesus show His love to the lady from Samaria?** (He talked to her and listened to her. He was kind to her.) **How can you show love to your friend?** Say: **Jesus loves all people, and He wants us to love all people too.** Sing "Jesus Loves Us Everyone" (page 60/track #50).

2. The Science-Math Bin: All the People of the World

Materials: plain white paper plates, people stickers (faces or full figures of different kinds of people)

Do: Give each child a paper plate. Ask the children to pretend the plate is a globe of the world. Ask them to stick different people stickers in a circle around the plate, then color sea and land in the center.

Discuss: Ask the children how people around the world might be different from them. (Language, clothing, food, transportation, holidays) **Does Jesus love people who are different from us? How did Jesus show His love to the lady from Samaria?** (He talked to her and listened to her. He was kind to her.) **How can you show love to your friend?** Say: **Jesus loves all people, and He wants us to love all people too.** Sing "Jesus Loves Us Everyone" (page 60/track #50).

3. The Look and Listen Bin: Being Friends

Materials: books and/or CDs/DVDs about friends and people of the world, CD/DVD player

You may use your own books and CDs/DVDs. The following are suggestions:
"Friends" and "Stone Soup" from PlaySongs: Tiny Treausres CD/DVD by Karyn Henley
The Rainbow Fish by Marcus Pfister
Stone Soup by Marcia Brown
My Friend and I by Lisa Jahn-Clough
The Mitten by Alvin Tresselt

© Karyn Henley. All rights reserved.

<u>Where are Maisy's Friends?</u> by Lucy Cousins
<u>Friends</u> by Helme Heine
<u>People</u> by Peter Spier
<u>Alfie Gives a Hand</u> by Shirley Hughes
<u>Will I Have a Friend</u> by Miriam Cohen

Do: Read the book(s) or let the children look at the pictures while you point out anything that demonstrates friendship with different people. Play any CDs or DVDs you've chosen, and describe how people are friends.

Discuss: Say: **Jesus loves all people, and He wants us to love all people too.**

4. **The Creative Movement Bin: Friends All Around**

   Materials: none

   Do: Encourage the children to copy you as you do the following song and action rhymes.

Sun Down   (track #77)
Children line up behind a leader, with their hands on the shoulder of the child in front of them. Guide the leader to march around the room. The others must follow.
Say: **Friends in the country,**
        Friends in town,
        Friends that are quiet,
        And friends that are loud.
        Friends that follow me
        All around
        When the sun comes up
        And at sun down.

When you say, "sun down," everyone squats. The leader goes to the back of the line and the second child becomes the leader.

See All the People   (to the tune of "Down By the Station"/track #71)
Ask the children to stand. Choose one to be the train engine.

> **Down by the station early in the morning,**
> **See all the people waiting for the train.**
> **The train comes along,**   (The "engine" passes by the standing children. Each
>   child he passes holds onto his waist and follows along.)
> **The people climb aboard,**
> **And chug, chug, choo, choo!**
> **We're all friends!**

Discuss: Say: **Jesus loves all people, and He wants us to love all people too.**

5. The Game Bin: Simon Says Colors

Materials: none

Do: Seat all the children in front of you. Tell them to look at the colors they are wearing. You will give them instructions according to colors. If you say their color, they are to do what you say. If you don't say their color, they don't do what you say. For example, if you say, "Red, jump up," all children who are wearing red should jump up. Any child who is not wearing red should stay seated.

Discuss: Point out that we are all different in some ways. We are all wearing different colors of clothing. Ask the children to point out other ways in which there are differences. Ask them to point out how everyone is alike. Say: **Jesus loves all people, and He wants us to love all people too.** Sing "Jesus Loves Us Everyone" (page 60/track #50).

6. The Snack Bin: Fruit Salad

Materials: one plastic zipper-locking bag for each child, bananas, a can of mandarin oranges, a can of fruit cocktail, kiwi fruit, blueberries, apples, grapes, a large bowl, a mixing spoon, a can opener and knife for teacher, plastic or paper picnic bowls, plastic spoons, paper towels, hand wipes

Note: Before class, peel and slice the apples and kiwi fruit and cut them into chunks. Open the cans of mandarin oranges and fruit cocktail. Place the sliced fruit as well as the canned fruit in plastic zipper-locking bags, one bag for each child. Save the bananas, and slice them later in class.

Do: Ask the children to wash their hands with wipes. Pray, thanking God that Jesus loves everyone, and thanking Him for the snack. Set out the large mixing bowl. Give each child a bag of fruit. Help each child open his or her bag and dump the contents into the big bowl. Slice bananas on top. Let each child take a turn stirring the fruit salad. Then serve each child a bowl of the fruit.

Discuss: As the children work, ask them to tell how each different ingredient of the fruit salad is different (flavor, color, texture) Say: **All the different parts mix together to make something very special. When different people get together and treat each other in loving ways, it can be very special. Jesus loves all people, and He wants us to love all people too.** Sing "Jesus Loves Us Everyone" (page 60/track #50). Ask how we can show love to others.

Heart Sample Pattern

Lesson 12

We Love and Worship Jesus

Memory Verse for the Quarter: "Grow knowing Jesus." 2 Peter 3:18, ICB, simplified

Scripture "God wants every knee to bow to Jesus." Philippians 2:10, ICB

Bible Story Mary puts perfume on Jesus' feet, John 12:1–8

Goal Learn that Mary showed Jesus she loved Him.
Learn that we can show Jesus we love and worship Him.

Today's Teacher Task
- Point out ways we worship and show our love to Jesus.
- Repeat as often as appropriate:
    Mary showed Jesus she loved Him.
    We can love and worship Jesus too.

INTRODUCTION

Materials: five paper plates, fresh mint, whole cloves, peel from four lemons, peel from three oranges, dried pineapple pieces, plastic sandwich bags, gift wrap ribbon

Do: Set out the paper plates. Put fresh mint on one, whole cloves on one, lemon peel on one, orange peel on one, and dried pineapple on one. As the children arrive, ask them to smell each of the different fragrances. Give each child a plastic sandwich bag. Ask the children to choose one piece from each plate to put into their bags to make potpourri. Tie the bags closed with ribbon. Tell the children they can take this home and use it as potpourri to make their homes smell good.

Discuss: As the children work, ask them to tell how each item smells. Ask: **If you had a campfire, what might you smell?** (smoke, something cooking over the fire - like hot dogs) **If you had a garden, what might you smell? What do you like to smell in your kitchen? What is your favorite smell?**

LARGE GROUP TIME
Sing "Come to the Circle" (page 6/track #9), and gather the children together in a large group.

Bible Story

Materials: a Bible marked at John 12, a bottle of cologne or perfume

Timesaver Option: the <u>Before I Dream Bedtime Bible Storybook</u> and/or the CD <u>Before I Dream: Lord I Love You</u>, a CD player

Do: If you use the Bible storybook, read the story "Sweet Perfume" or play the story "Sweet Perfume" from the CD, and play the following song, "I Love You, Lord."

If you do not use the Bible storybook, open the Bible to John 12 and say, **Here's where the Bible tells about a lady named Mary. Mary had a sister named Martha. One day Jesus went to dinner at Mary and Martha's house. Martha served the food. But Mary took a bottle of perfume.** Open a bottle of cologne and let the children smell it. **Mary poured perfume on Jesus' feet.** As you tell this, put a little on each child's feet or ankles. **Mary did this to show Jesus how much she loved Him.**

Discuss: Ask: **How can we show Jesus we love Him?** (We can try to be like Him, being kind and loving to others. We can worship Him.) **Worship means "to bow." When we bow to someone, we are treating them as being very important. Sometimes we bow when we worship. What are some other ways to worship? Let's worship Jesus now.**

Songs and Movement

Sing "Lord, We Bow and Worship You" to the tune of "Twinkle, Twinkle Little Star" (track #57).

Lord, we bow and worship You.	(bow)
You are loving; You are true.	(hands over heart)
You're our great and pow'rful King,	(make "strong arm" muscles)
Ruler over everything.	(arms outstretched)
Lord, we bow and worship You.	(bow)
You are loving; You are true.	(hands over heart)

Sing the memory verse song, "Growing Knowing Jesus" (page 6/track #28).

Prayer

Ask the children to fold their hands and pray the words after you:
Dear God, Your Son Jesus is wonderful! We love and worship Him. Amen.

© Karyn Henley. All rights reserved.

EXPLORE-A-BINS
Choose from these activities. Use them in the order that best suits your needs.

1. The Art Bin: Worship Pictures

Materials: paper, preschool washable liquid paint, paintbrushes, smocks, newspaper or a plastic tablecloth, packets of unsweetened powdered drink mix in colors that match the paints (for example, yellow drink mix for yellow paint, etc.)

Do: Before class, mix the powdered drink mixes into the paints that most nearly match their color. This gives the paints a scent. Cover the work surface with newspaper or plastic tablecloth. Put smocks on the children. Give each child a piece of paper and a paintbrush. Say: The Bible says, **"Everything you say and everything you do should all be done for Jesus your Lord"** (Colossians 3:17, ICB). **We are going to paint pictures for Jesus and hang them on the wall.** Now ask the children to paint whatever they want to paint for Jesus.

Discuss: As the children paint, point out that doing things for Jesus is one way to worship Him and show our love for Him. Also, ask the children to smell the different colors. Ask: **What does this color smell like? What did Mary have in her jar? What did she do with the perfume? Why?** Say: **Mary showed Jesus she loved Him. We can love and worship Jesus too.** Sing "Lord, We Bow and Worship You" (page 66/track #57).

2. The Science-Math Bin: What's That Smell?

Materials: cinnamon in a small zipper-locking bag, a bottle of vanilla, a jar of peanut butter, bananas, cheese in a zipper-locking bag, hand wipes, a box or bag to hide all these in

Do: Ask the children to close and cover their eyes. Open the cinnamon bag. Let each child sniff it, but not say what it is. Then ask, **What's that smell?** They can all say what they think it is. Then let them see it. Do the same with the vanilla, peanut butter, banana, and cheese. Then do the same with hand wipes. After they've sniffed these, ask them to clean their hands with the wipes. Give each child half of a banana to eat.

Discuss: Ask: **How did you know it was peanut butter? How did you know I had a banana? What is your favorite smell? Our noses have special parts in them that smell things. Mary put perfume on Jesus' feet, knowing that He would like the smell. It was a way for Mary to show Jesus she loved Him. We can love and worship Jesus too.** Sing "Lord, We Bow and Worship You" (page 66/track #57).

3. The Look and Listen Bin: Worship

Materials: books and/or CDs/DVDs about worship, and celebration CD/DVD player

You may use your own books and CDs/DVDs. The following are suggestions:
Give Thanks to the Lord or Let's Make a Joyful Noise by Karma Wilson
Clap Hands by Helen Oxenbury
Story "David Praises God" from My Learn to Pray Bible by Karyn Henley
"Sweet Perfume" story from Before I Dream Bedtime Bible Storybook by Karyn Henley
"Sweet Perfume" story and "I Love You, Lord" song from Before I Dream: Lord I Love You CD by Karyn Henley
"Great Big God" from PlaySongs: Grow, Grow, Grow CD/DVD by Karyn Henley
"Praise Him, Praise Him" from PlaySongs: Tiny Treausres CD/DVD by Karyn Henley
"Praise the Lord" from PlaySongs: I Feel Like a Giggle CD/DVD by Karyn Henley

Do: Read the book(s) or let the children look at the pictures while you point out anything that has to do with worship. Play any CDs or DVDs you've chosen.

Discuss: Say: **Mary showed Jesus she loved Him. We can love and worship Jesus too.**

4. The Creative Movement Bin: Worshiping God

Materials: streamers, rhythm instruments*

*Note: You can make shakers by putting uncooked rice or dry beans or paper clips into paper lunch sacks and stapling the sacks closed.

PlaySongs by Karyn Henley - CD/DVD Suggestions:
"I Like to Play Music" and "Thank You March" from Noah's Zoo
"Psalm 150," from Five Little Ladybugs
"Rock-a-My Soul" from I Feel Like a Giggle

Do: Encourage the children to play their instruments as you sing together or play the songs from the CDs/DVDs.

If you prefer not to use recorded music, you can sing the following song(s) as the children march, clap, wave their streamers and/or shake the bags they made.

Joyful Noise   (to the tune of "Oh Where Have You Been, Billy Boy?"/track #56)
   Oh, make a joyful noise to the Lord, all the earth,
   Oh, make a joyful noise to the Lord.
   Oh, make a joyful noise
   All you girls and all you boys,
   Oh, come make a joyful, joyful noise.

Praise Band   (to the tune of "Twinkle, Twinkle, Little Star"/track #58)
   Marching, marching, everyone,
   Marching, marching, here we come.
   When we march, we praise our God,
   Thanking Him for all He's done.
   Marching, marching, everyone,
   Marching, marching, here we come.

Discuss: Say: **Mary showed Jesus she loved Him. We can love and worship Jesus too.**

5. The Game Bin: The Worship Chair

Materials: nature pictures cut out of magazines or coloring books, a praise CD and CD player

Do: Put the chairs in a circle, one chair for each child. Stack the pictures under one of the chairs. This is the Worship Chair. Now ask the children to stand outside the circle of chairs. When you play the music, the children should march around the outside of the circle. When you stop the music, the children should stop. Then they sit in the chair they are standing behind. The child who sits in the Worship Chair should reach under the chair and take out the picture on the top of the stack. He shows the picture to the group and tells what it is. Say: **We worship Jesus, because He is the King over all the (whatever the picture was).** Ask the children to say with you, **You are great, Jesus! We worship you!** Ask the child in the Worship Chair to place the picture in the center of the circle, then start the game again.

Discuss: Say: **Mary showed Jesus she loved Him. We can love and worship Jesus too.** Sing "Lord, We Bow and Worship You" (page 66/track #57).

6. The Snack Bin: Cheese and Fruit

Materials: three different kinds of cheese (cheddar, a smoky-smelling cheese like Provolone, and Swiss or Parmesan cheese), a knife for teacher, apple slices, juice, paper plates and cups, paper towels, hand wipes

Do: Ask the children to wash their hands with wipes. Pray, telling God how wonderful His Son Jesus is, and thank Him for the snack. Ask the children to smell the cheese as you give each of them a small square of each kind of cheese.

Discuss: Describe the different smells: creamy, smoky, tangy, sweet, etc. Say: **To show her love, Mary gave Jesus something that smelled good. What was it? How can we show our love to Jesus?** Say: **Mary showed Jesus she loved Him. We can love and worship Jesus too.** Sing "Lord, We Bow and Worship You" (page 66/track #57).

Lesson 13

Jesus Will Come Back Someday

Memory Verse for the Quarter: "Grow knowing Jesus." 2 Peter 3:18, ICB, simplified

Scripture "He (Jesus) will come back in the same way you saw him go."
Acts 1:11, ICB

Bible Story Jesus' ascension, Luke 24:50-53, Acts 1:7-11

Goal Learn that Jesus went up into heaven, and someday He will come back.

Today's Teacher Task
- Point out clouds and sky.
- Repeat as often as appropriate:
    Jesus went up into heaven.
    Someday He will come back again.

INTRODUCTION

Materials: a long piece of butcher paper, tape or temporary plastic adhesive (like Plasti-Tak or Tak 'n Stik), crayons and/or markers

Do: Hang the piece of butcher paper across one wall, or stretch it out on the floor. As the children arrive, assign each of them a section of paper to work on. They will be drawing a landscape that includes a hill, empty crosses, and an empty tomb. Assign each child something specific to draw, such as the rocks around the tomb, the clouds, the sun, the crosses, the grass, flowers, birds, etc.

Discuss: As the children work, ask: **What happened to Jesus at the cross? What happened to Him at the tomb?** Say: **After Jesus came alive again, He met with His**

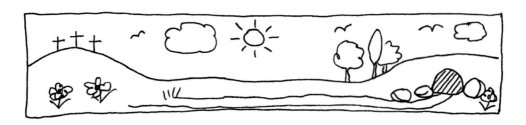

friends. He ate with them and talked with them. How do you think Jesus' friends felt about Jesus?

LARGE GROUP TIME
Sing "Come to the Circle" (page 6/track #9), and gather the children together in a large group.
Bible Story

> **Materials:** a Bible marked at Acts 1, the Jesus figure and cloud figure copied and cut out from page 69
>
> **Timesaver Option:** the <u>Before I Dream Bedtime Bible Storybook</u>

Do: If you use the Bible storybook, read the story "Hidden by the Clouds."

If you do not use the Bible storybook, open the Bible to Acts 1 and say, **Here's where the Bible tells about a day when Jesus took His friends out to the countryside.** Ask the children to pretend to be Jesus' friends who were with Him that day. Lead them around the room, walking. **Out of Jerusalem they walked. Out into the countryside, almost to the town of Bethany.** Ask the children to sit around you. Take out the cloud figure and hold it high with one hand. Hold the Jesus figure in the other hand. Say: **Jesus told His friends, "You will tell lots of other people about me." Then an amazing thing happened. While His friends were watching, Jesus went up, up, up into the air.** Raise the Jesus figure. **His friends watched until He was hidden by the clouds.** Hide the Jesus figure behind the cloud in your other hand. **Show me what you think Jesus' friends' faces might have looked like as they watched this. Suddenly two men were standing there beside them. These men said, "Why are you looking up into the sky? Jesus went into heaven. Someday He will come back the same way He left. Then Jesus' friends went back to the city, amazed and happy.**

Discuss: Ask: **Does anyone know exactly when Jesus will come back? Only God knows. But when He comes back, we will get to be with Him forever, and He will get to be with us forever!**

Songs and Movement
Sing "Jesus Will Come Back" to the tune of "The Farmer in the Dell" (track #53).

Oh, Jesus will come back,	(arms outstretched overhead, swaying)
Oh, Jesus will come back,	
Coming, coming through the sky,	
Oh, Jesus will come back.	
Then I will clap for Him,	(clap)
Then I will clap for Him,	
Jesus will come back again,	
And I will clap for Him.	

© Karyn Henley. All rights reserved.

Then I will jump for joy, (jump)
Then I will jump for joy,
Jesus will come back again,
And I will jump for joy.

Then I will bow to Him, (bow)
Then I will bow to Him,
Jesus will come back again,
And I will bow to Him.

Sing the memory verse song, "Growing Knowing Jesus" (page 6/track #28).

Prayer
Ask the children to fold their hands and pray the words after you:
Dear God, Thank you that Jesus is coming back someday. Amen.

EXPLORE-A-BINS
Choose from these activities. Use them in the order that best suits your needs.

1. The Art Bin: Ascension Mobiles

Materials: cardboard or posterboard strips 2-inches x 8-inches, tape, two 6-inch strings for each child, one 8-inch string for each child, one 18-inch string for each child, one Jesus figure and two cloud figures for each child copied and cut out from page 69, cotton, glue

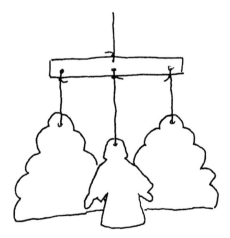

Do: Give each child a cardboard strip and two 6-inch strings. Help the children tape the strings to the strip, one string at each end as shown. Now give each child one 8-inch string and help them tape that string in the center as shown. Give each child an 18-inch string to tape from the top of the strip as shown. Now give each child one Jesus figure and two cloud figures. Help them tape the Jesus figure to the middle 8-inch string. Help them tape the cloud figures to the two 6-inch strings. Then ask the children to glue cotton balls to the clouds.

(To save time in class, tape the strings to each strip of cardboard before class. Let the children tape the figures on in class.)

Discuss: As the children work, ask: **What did Jesus tell his friends before He went**

back to heaven? How did He go into heaven? What did His friends do then? Say: **Jesus went up into heaven. Someday He will come back again.** Sing "Jesus Will Come Back" (page 71/track #53).

2. **The Science-Math Bin: Clouds**

   Materials: cans of shaving cream, large pieces of light blue construction paper, liquid preschool washable watercolor paints, one copy of the "Clouds" page (page 70), paper towels, hand wipes

   Do: Show the children the clouds on the "Clouds" page. Read their names and tell what kinds of weather we are most likely to have when these kinds of clouds are in the sky. Then give each child a piece of paper. Squirt a "cloud" of shaving cream on the paper, and ask the children to choose a cloud shape from the "Clouds" page. Ask them to try to make that same shape with the shaving cream by swirling it around on the paper. Add more shaving cream if necessary. Add drips of different colors of paint to make the clouds look like rain clouds, or to make them look like a sunset.

   Discuss: Tell the children that clouds are made of water vapor and dust particles. Ask: **Are all clouds the same shape? What happened with the cloud in our story? What did Jesus' friends do? What did the two men standing with them say? What will Jesus do when He comes back?** (Take us to be with Him.) Say: **Jesus went up into heaven. Someday He will come back again.** Sing "Jesus Will Come Back" (page 71/track #53).

3. **The Look and Listen Bin: Into the Clouds**

   Materials: books and/or CDs/DVDs about clouds and Jesus and praise, CD/DVD player

   You may use your own books and CDs/DVDs. The following are suggestions:
   The Cloud Book by Tomie dePaola
   Little Cloud by Eric Carle
   Clap Hands by Helen Oxenbury
   Give Thanks to the Lord or Let's Make a Joyful Noise by Karma Wilson
   "Hidden by the Clouds" story from Before I Dream Bedtime Bible Storybook by Karyn Henley
   "Great Big God" from PlaySongs: Grow, Grow, Grow CD/DVD by Karyn Henley
   "Praise Him, Praise Him" from PlaySongs: Tiny Treausres CD/DVD by Karyn Henley
   "Praise the Lord" from PlaySongs: I Feel Like a Giggle CD/DVD by Karyn Henley

   Do: Read the book(s) or let the children look at the pictures while you point out anything that has to do with clouds or Jesus or praise. Play any CDs or DVDs you've chosen.

   Discuss: Say: **Jesus went up into heaven. Someday He will come back again.**

4. The Creative Movement Bin: Clouds

Materials: polyester fiberfill (stuffing used for pillows), optional: <u>PlaySongs: Five Little Ladybugs</u> CD/DVD by Karyn Henley, CD/DVD player

Do: Play "I Am a Little Cloud" from the CD or DVD. If you choose not to use the music, lead the children in the motions to the song "Jesus Will Come Back" (page 71/track #53). Then give each child a large handful of fiberfill so each child can pretend to be a cloud. Ask the children to join you in the motions to the following song:

<u>Clouds Around the World</u>   (to the tune of "Row, Row, Row Your Boat"/track #8)
   Clouds around the world,
   'Way up in the sky,
   Jesus is coming, He's coming again!
   Praise to God Most High!

The first time through the song, ask the children to march around the room, waving their fiberfill clouds. As you repeat the song, ask the children to move around the room in different ways: jump, tiptoe, skip, etc.

Discuss: Say: **Jesus went up into heaven. Someday He will come back again.**

5. The Game Bin: Hidden in the Clouds

Materials: a white or blue bedsheet

Do: Spread the bedsheet on the floor. Ask the children to stand around the edges of the sheet and hold the edge in front of them with both hands. Tell them that this sheet will be the cloud. The cloud is going to hide someone. When you say, "Up," the children should raise their hands high, bringing the sheet up. Call out the name of one child. That child should run under the sheet quickly and sit. Let the sheet drift back down over the child. Ask, "Who is the cloud hiding now?" Then say, "Up." Call the child's name again. The child should crawl back out before the sheet comes back down. Repeat this, calling different children to hide in the cloud each time.

Discuss: Ask: **Who was hidden by a cloud in our story? How did it happen?** Say: **Jesus went up into heaven. Someday He will come back again.** Sing "Jesus Will Come Back" (page 71/track #53).

6. The Snack Bin: Cloud Crackers

Materials: graham crackers, non-dairy whipped topping, plastic picnic spoons, juice, paper plates and cups, paper towels, hand wipes

Do: Ask the children to wash their hands with wipes. Pray, thanking God that

Jesus will come back someday. Give each child a paper plate, a spoon, and a square of graham cracker. Ask the children to put a big scoop of whipped topping on their graham crackers. Ask them if this reminds them of anything in the story. Point out that it looks like a cloud. Ask them to eat their cloud snacks.

Discuss: Ask: **Are all clouds the same shape? What happened with the cloud in our story? What did Jesus' friends do? What did the two men standing with them say? Say: Jesus went up into heaven. Someday He will come back again.** Sing "Jesus Will Come Back" (page 71/track #53).

Jesus and Cloud Figures

Clouds

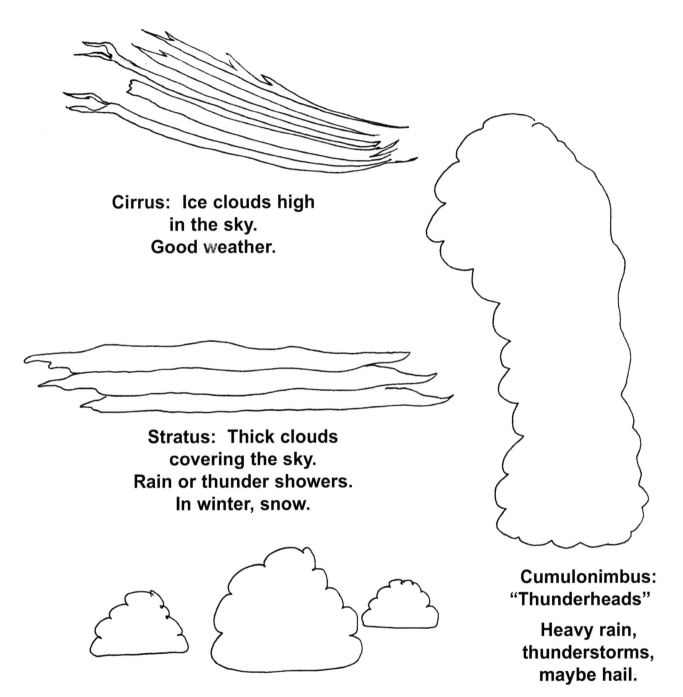

About Materials

As you consider materials, think creatively. You may not have to purchase all materials. Try posting a needs list outside the door of your room, or in the church bulletin, or in postcards mailed to parents. Ask parents and other church members to donate or purchase some of these items for you.

Here are some general guidelines from the American Academy of Pediatrics for choosing toys:
- Avoid toys that shoot small objects into the air.
- Avoid toys that make loud or shrill noises.
- Look for sturdy toys.
- Parts (eyes, nose) on stuffed animals should be sewed on securely.
- Stuffed animals should be machine-washable.
- Look at the seams on dolls, stuffed animals, and rattles to make sure they are secure.
- Avoid toys stuffed with pellet-type material.
- Avoid toys with sharp edges and toys that seem fragile.

Some good toys for fours are:
- sturdy dolls
- CD player
- simple puppets
- crayons, play dough
- picture books
- toy telephones
- tea party utensils
- dress-up clothes
- transportation toys
- non-toxic finger paints
- chalkboard and chalk
- housekeeping toys
- dollhouse and toy figures
- building blocks
- simple puzzles with large pieces

A Week-by-Week List of Materials You Will Need

NOTE: Many of the recommended books and videos are the same as those recommended for 3's and 5/K Curriculum. If these classes are using the PlaySongs curriculum, you may want to share these resources with them to save expense. It is very probable that the materials will not be needed by both classes at the same time, except for the recommended CDs/DVDs.

Week 1:
- a board about 1' wide by 3' long
- a roll of heavy-duty paper towels
- postable sticky notes
- a Bible with a bookmark at Matthew 13:55
- two bricks or sturdy blocks the same size
- tape or reusable adhesive (Plasti-tak or Tac 'n stik)
- a pen

The Art Bin:
- paper
- paper towels
- preschool washable liquid paint
- hand wipes
- paper plates

The Science-Math Bin:
- different sizes of shoes, socks, shirts, hats (some for babies, some for older children)

The Look and Listen Bin:
- books, CDs and/or DVDs about growing
- CD/DVD player, if necessary

Suggestions:
>Here Are My Hands by Bill Martin, Jr. and John Archambault
>The Carrot Seed by Ruth Krauss
>Is It Larger? Is It Smaller? by Tana Hoban
>I Can Fly by Ruth Krauss
>My Thank You Bible Stories & Songs CD by Karyn Henley
>PlaySongs: Grow, Grow, Grow, CD/DVD by Karyn Henley
>PlaySongs: Tiny Treasures, CD/DVD by Karyn Henley
>PlaySongs: I Feel Like a Giggle, CD/DVD by Karyn Henley

The Creative Movement Bin:
- a bright light, lamp, or slide projector
- option: CD and player
- sheets to put over any windows to darken the room if necessary

The Game Bin:
- five different colors of balloons
- tape
- a measuring tape or yardstick
- a jump rope

The Snack Bin:
- mandarin orange segments
- bananas
- apple slices
- cheese squares
- juice
- paper plates and cups
- paper towels
- hand wipes
- knife for teacher to use

Week 2:
- balloons
- streamers
- tape and/or plastic temporary adhesive (Plasti-Tak or Tak 'n Stik)
- a Bible with a bookmark at John 2
- a plastic pitcher (preferably not transparent)
- a packet of pre-sweetened red or purple powdered drink mix
- a long handled stirring spoon
- water
- paper towels
- a 2-cup lliquid measuring cup
- paper cups

Timesaver Option: the Before I Dream Bedtime Bible Storybook by Karyn Henley

The Art Bin:
- newspapers or a plastic tablecloth
- a bucket or tub or sink of water
- powdered unsweetened drink mix of a variety of colors
- plastic picnic bowls
- plastic spoons
- paper towels

The Science-Math Bin:
- 1/2 cup of whipping cream
- a 1-quart plastic jar with a tight-fitting lid
- paper towels
- crackers
- salt
- butter knife
- spoon
- hand wipes

The Look and Listen Bin:
- books, CDs and/or DVDs about Jesus, or about parties, or about food
- CD/DVD player, if necessary
- Suggestions:
    Jesus Loves Me by Debby Anderson
    Water, Water Everywhere by Julie Aigner-Clark
    Do You Know About Water? by Mae Blacker Freeman
    Spot Bakes a Cake by Eric Hill
    Bear's All-Night Party by Bill Harley
    Rabbit's Pajama Party by Stuart J. Murphy
    PlaySongs: Grow, Grow, Grow CD/DVD by Karyn Henley
    PlaySongs: Tiny Treasures CD/DVD by Karyn Henley
    Before I Dream Bedtime Bible Storybook by Karyn Henley

The Creative Movement Bin:
- a blue sheet, towel, pillowcase, or scarf

The Game Bin:
- a basket or box   - a towel or cloth that will cover the basket or box
- a variety of household items that are familiar to four-year-olds (comb, CD, crayon, small
    cup, spoon, small toy, etc.)

The Snack Bin:
- 5 medium-sized lemons   - 5 cups cold water   - 1 cup sugar
- a knife for teacher's use - a pitcher   - measuring cups and spoons
- a long-handled spoon   - paper cups   - paper towels
- hand wipes   - optional: crackers

Week 3:
- boxes large enough for the children to sit in (or use classroom chairs)
- crayons   - option: PlaySongs: Down By the Station CD and CD player
- a Bible with a bookmark at Matthew 9

The Art Bin:
- newspapers or a plastic tablecloth   - one white handkerchief for each child
- fabric paints or markers

The Science-Math Bin:
- large pieces of manila paper
- two small boxes for each child (single-serving milk cartons, cereal boxes, juice boxes, or
    yogurt containers work well)
- glue or tape or plastic temporary adhesive (Plasti-Tak or Tak 'n Stik)
- crayons   - a ruler   - optional: small toy vehicles

The Look and Listen Bin:
- books, CDs and/or DVDs about friends   - CD/DVD player, if necessary

- Suggestions:
    - The Rainbow Fish by Marcus Pfister
    - Stone Soup by Marcia Brown
    - My Friend and I by Lisa Jahn-Clough
    - The Mitten by Alvin Tresselt
    - Bear's Busy Family by Stella Blackstone
    - Friends by Helme Heine
    - Where are Maisy's Friends? by Lucy Cousins
    - Alfie Gives a Hand by Shirley Hughes
    - Will I Have a Friend by Miriam Cohen
    - Dear God, Thank You for Friends by Annie Fitzgerald & Ken Abraham
    - PlaySongs: Tiny Treausres CD/DVD by Karyn Henley
    - PlaySongs: Grow, Grow, Grow CD/DVD by Karyn Henley

The Creative Movement Bin: - none

The Game Bin:
- magazine pictures of a variety of nature scenes   - a box or bag

The Snack Bin:
- apple slices   - cheese slices   - juice   - paper plates and cups
- paper towels   - hand wipes

Week 4:
- play dough (To make play dough, mix 1 part water, 1 part salt, and 3 parts flour.)
- paper plates   - small rocks/gravel/sand   - string
- small twigs and plant stems with small leaves   - tape
- a Bible with a bookmark at Matthew 6
- birds made according to the pattern and instructions on page 23
- flowers (real or artificial)   - one or more vases

Timesaver Option: the Before I Dream Bedtime Bible Storybook and/or the Before I Dream: In Jesus' Arms CD, a CD player

The Art Bin:
- paper plates   - glue   - shredded coconut
- yellow food coloring   - mixing bowl   - mixing spoon
- jelly beans or speckled "bird's egg" candies   - paper towels
- hand wipes

The Science-Math Bin:
- newspaper or plastic tablecloth   - two small plants in pots   - paper towels
- paper   - crayons

The Look and Listen Bin:
- books, CDs/DVDs about plants and birds - a CD/DVD player if necessary
- Suggestions:
    - Are You My Mother? by P.D. Eastman
    - The Carrot Seed by Ruth Krauss
    - Make Way for Ducklings by Robert McCloskey
    - Planting a Rainbow by Lois Ehlert
    - The Story about Ping by Flack and Wiese
    - The Little Duck by Judy Dunn

        Growing Vegetable Soup by Lois Ehlert
        This Year's Garden by Cynthis Rylant
        From Seed to Plant by Gail Gibbons
        7 Days of Creation by Mindy MacDonald
        About Birds: A Guide for Children by Cathryn Sill
        Tell Me About God by Karyn Henley
        My First Hymnal CD by Karyn Henley
        PlaySongs: Down By the Station CD/DVD by Karyn Henley
        PlaySongs: Noah's Zoo CD/DVD by Karyn Henley
        PlaySongs: Grow,Grow, Grow CD/DVD by Karyn Henley
        PlaySongs: Tiny Treausres CD/DVD by Karyn Henley

The Creative Movement Bin:
- optional: CDs/DVDs with animal songs, CD/DVD player
    PlaySongs by Karyn Henley - CD/DVD Suggestions:
        Down By the Station   I Feel Like a Giggle
        Five Little Ladybugs   Grow, Grow, Grow

The Game Bin: - none

The Snack Bin:
- carrot sticks   - apple slices   - boiled eggs   - juice
- knife for teacher   - paper plates and cups   - paper towels   - hand wipes

Week 5:
- blocks   - cotton ball   - ten index cards   - marker
- a Bible with a bookmark at Luke 15

Timesaver Option: the Before I Dream Bedtime Bible Storybook and/or the Before I Dream: Dream of Heaven CD by Karyn Henley, CD player

The Art Bin:
- white paper plates   - crayons or markers   - tape or stapler and staples
- two sheep ears for each child (copied and cut out from page 29)
- glue   - cotton balls

The Science-Math Bin:
- a pillowcase or grocery bag
- a variety of objects that can be handled by children (These should be objects that do not last a long time: a banana, balloon, toy, sock, toothbrush, paper, toothpaste, plastic spoon, candle, etc.)

The Look and Listen Bin:
- books and/or CDs/DVDs about sheep or Jesus' love and care
- CD/DVD player, if necessary

Suggestions:
> Jesus Loves Me, Jesus Loves the Little Children, or Jesus is With Me by
> > Debby Anderson
> Sheep in a Jeep, Sheep in a Shop, Sheep in a Ship, or Sheep Takes a Hike by
> > Nancy E. Shaw
> PlaySongs: Noah's Zoo CD/DVD by Karyn Henley
> PlaySongs: I Feel Like a Giggle CD/DVD by Karyn Henley
> My Thank You Bible Stories & Songs CD by Karyn Henley
> Before I Dream: Dream of Heaven CD by Karyn Henley

The Creative Movement Bin:
- optional: PlaySongs: Five Little Ladybugs CD/DVD by Karyn Henley
- CD/DVD player

The Game Bin: - a jump rope

The Snack Bin:
- some peanuts in the shell
- 1 Tbs. peanut oil, crackers
- mixing spoon
- paper plates and cups
- 2 cups shelled roasted peanuts
- a blender
- measuring cups and spoons
- paper towels
- 1/2 tsp. salt
- mixing bowl
- juice
- hand wipes

Week 6:
- paper lunch sacks
- dried beans
- salt
- wide plastic tape (any color)
- uncooked dry rice
- pennies
- a stapler and staples
- a CD of praise music
- paper clips
- cotton balls
- a Bible with a bookmark at Matthew 21
- one palm leaf cut out of green paper for each child, and one for yourself (pattern on
    page 36)

The Art Bin:
- one white styrene "hot" cup for each child
- black permanent markers
- one or two paper plates
- brown crayons
- glue
- brown construction paper donkey ears
  (pattern on page 32)

The Science-Math Bin:
- lunch bag shakers from the introductory activity

The Look and Listen Bin:
- books and/or CDs/DVDs about Palm Sunday, Easter, praise and singing
- CD/DVD player, if necessary
- Suggestions:
> PlaySongs: Five Little Ladybugs CD/DVD by Karyn Henley
> L-O-V-E, a PlaySongs book about Jesus' death and resurrection by Karyn Henley
> PlaySongs: Tiny Treasures CD/DVD by Karyn Henley

PlaySongs: Noah's Zoo CD/DVD by Karyn Henley
Hurry, Hurry! by Mary Manz Simon   Easter ABC's by Isabel Anders
Little Colt's Palm Sunday by Michelle Medlock Adams
The Story of Easter by Aileen Fisher   J is for Jesus by Debbie Trafton O'Neal
My First Hymnal, CD by Karyn Henley

The Creative Movement Bin:
- rhythm instruments from the introductory activity   - CDs/DVDs to sing and play along with
- CD/DVD player
- Suggestions:
    PlaySongs: Noah's Zoo by Karyn Henley
    PlaySongs: Five Little Ladybugs by Karyn Henley
    PlaySongs: I Feel Like a Giggle by Karyn Henley

The Game Bin: - a paper palm leaf for each child (from story time)

The Snack Bin:
- a sheet or tablecloth   - animal crackers   - juice   - paper towels
- wipes

Week 7:
- one cross shape cut from paper for each child (pattern on page 42)
- hole puncher   - one 14-inch length of string or yarn for each child
- uncooked hollow cylindrical pasta (ziti or rigatoni)
- a Bible with a marker at Matthew 27
- a cross cut out of a large piece of construction paper or poster board
- tape or a thumb tack or temporary plastic adhesive (like Plasti-Tak or Tak 'n Stik)
- a sheet   - a pillow or large circle cut from poster board
- a flashlight
Timesaver Option: the Before I Dream Bedtime Bible Storybook

The Art Bin:
- newspaper or a plastic tablecloth   - rectangular sponges into cross shapes
- light blue construction paper   - one or more paper plates
- brown washable preschool paint   - paper towels
- hand wipes

The Science-Math Bin: - none

The Look and Listen Bin:
- books and/or CDs/DVDs about Palm Sunday, Easter, praise and singing
- CD/DVD player, if necessary
- Suggestions:
Mary and the Empty Tomb by Alice Joyce Davidson
        He is Alive by Helen Haidle   The Easter Story by Brian Wildsmith
        Hurry, Hurry! by Mary Manz Simon   Easter ABC's by Isabel Anders

J is for Jesus by Debbie Trafton O'Neal   The Story of Easter by Aileen Fisher
My First Hymnal, CD by Karyn Henley
Before I Dream Bedtime Bible Storybook by Karyn Henley
PlaySongs: Five Little Ladybugs CD/DVD by Karyn Henley
L-O-V-E, a PlaySongs book about Jesus' death and resurrection by Karyn Henley
PlaySongs: Tiny Treasures CD/DVD by Karyn Henley

The Game Bin: - none

The Snack Bin:
- bread or sliced biscuits   - jelly in a squirt bottle   - juice
- paper plates and cups   - paper towels   - hand wipes

Week 8:
- hand towels or bath towels or pillowcases or baby blankets   - stuffed animals
- a Bible with a bookmark at Luke 6   - toy doctors' kit

The Art Bin:
- a cap front and arm band for each child copied and cut out from pattern, page 42
- red crayons   - a stapler and staples   - tape
- a 1-inch x 20-inch strip of construction paper or posterboard for each child

The Science-Math Bin:
- toy doctor kits   - a real stethoscope if possible
- adhesive strip bandages of different sizes   - baby dolls, pillows and blankets
- baby beds or boxes

The Look and Listen Bin:
- books and/or CDs/DVDs about being sick or about Jesus
- CD/DVD player, if necessary
    My Thank You Bible Stories & Songs CD by Karyn Henley
    Jesus Loves the Little Children, Jesus is With Me, or Jesus Loves Me by
        Debby Anderson
    Doctor Maisy by Lucy Cousins
    Bear Feels Sick by Karma Wilson
    My Learn to Pray Bible by Karyn Henley
    PlaySongs: Grow, Grow, Grow CD/DVD by Karyn Henley

The Creative Movement Bin: - none

The Game Bin: - a clean, empty plastic medicine bottle

The Snack Bin:
- blueberries   - vanilla yogurt   - plastic spoons
- paper bowls   - paper towels   - hand wipes

© Karyn Henley. All rights reserved.

Week 9:
- one bendable drinking straw for each child
- scissors for teacher
- long chenille wire (pipe cleaners)
- play dough (Note: You can use store-bought play dough, or make it yourself, or let the children make it as part of the activity. To make play dough, mix 1 part water, 1 part salt, and 3 parts flour.)
- a Bible with a bookmark at Luke 13
- the figures the children made in the introductory activity (Note: If you didn't do the introductory activity, you may make one figure for yourself before class to help you tell the story, or you may make one for each child and hand them out before the story so the children can help tell the story, each child with a figure.)

The Art Bin:
- a 4 1/2-inch long cardboard tube for each child from a roll of toilet paper or paper towels or gift wrap (Note: You can make tubes by rolling paper into a cylinder and stapling or taping it.)
- markers
- yarn or cotton balls or fringed construction paper
- glue
- small adhesive bandages

The Science-Math Bin:
- strips of gauze bandages and a variety of other bandages

The Look and Listen Bin:
- books and/or CDs/DVDs about being sick or about praising Jesus
- CD/DVD player, if necessary
- Suggestions:
    My Thank You Bible Stories & Songs CD by Karyn Henley
    Jesus Loves Me, Jesus Loves the Little Children, or Jesus is With Me by
        Debby Anderson
    Doctor Maisy by Lucy Cousins
    Bear Feels Sick by Karma Wilson
    My First Hymnal, CD by Karyn Henley
    Give Thanks to the Lord or Let's Make a Joyful Noise by Karma Wilson
    My Learn to Pray Bible by Karyn Henley
  Any of the following from Playsongs series by Karyn Henley:
    Noah's Zoo CD/DVD
    I Feel Like a Giggle CD/DVD
    Grow, Grow, Grow CD/DVD
    Down by the Station CD/DVD
    Tiny Treausres CD/DVD

The Creative Movement Bin:
- rhythm instruments or paper cups with the bottoms punched out
- CDs/DVDs to sing and play along with
- CD/DVD player
- Suggestions:
    PlaySongs: Noah's Zoo by Karyn Henley
    PlaySongs: Five Little Ladybugs by Karyn Henley
    PlaySongs: I Feel Like a Giggle by Karyn Henley

The Game Bin: - none

The Snack Bin:
- English muffins
- whipped cream cheese
- hand wipes
- tubes of ready made red frosting or red jelly in a squirt bottle
- juice
- paper plates and cups
- plastic picnic spoons
- paper towels

Week 10:
- paper plates
- scissors for teacher
- tape
- crayons
- a Bible with a bookmark at Mark 14
- a blue bedsheet or tablecloth

The Art Bin:
- blue play dough (Note: If you want to make a soft play dough, mix 1 cup of vegetable oil, 6 cups of flour, and 1 cup of water. Add blue food coloring.)
- paper plates
- paper towels
- optional: boat stickers

The Science-Math Bin:
- a coffee cup
- water
- pennies
- a bath towel
- paper towels

The Look and Listen Bin:
- books and/or CDs/DVDs about boats or lakes or Jesus' love and care
- CD/DVD player, if necessary
- Suggestions:
    Jesus Loves Me, Jesus Loves the Little Children, or Jesus is With Me
        by Debby Anderson
    Boats by Byron Barton   Nicole's Boat by Allen Morgan
    Busy Boats by Tony Mitton & Ant Parker   Mr. Gumpy's Outing by John Burningham
    My Learn To Pray Bible by Karyn Henley
    PlaySongs: Noah's Zoo CD/DVD by Karyn Henley

The Creative Movement Bin:
- a 1' x 2' strip of blue sheer fabric or scarf for each child, or a blue streamer for each child

The Game Bin: - none

The Snack Bin:
- sliced English muffins
- whipped cream cheese with blue food coloring mixed in it
- juice
- plastic spoons
- paper plates and cups
- paper towels
- hand wipes

Week 11:
- heart shapes cut from different patterns of gift wrap (two hearts from each kind of wrap (heart sample pattern is on page 64)
- Option: Instead of gift wrap, you can cut hearts from different colors of construction paper, two hearts of each color.

- a Bible with a bookmark at John 4
- a real pitcher of water
- boxes or blocks
- paper cups

The Art Bin:
- one large piece of manila paper for each child
- crayons

The Science-Math Bin:
- plain white paper plates
- people stickers (faces or full figures of different kinds of people)

The Look and Listen Bin:
- books and/or CDs/DVDs about friends and people of the world
- CD/DVD player, if necessary
- Suggestions:
    PlaySongs: Tiny Treausres CD/DVD by Karyn Henley
    The Rainbow Fish by Marcus Pfister   Stone Soup by Marcia Brown
    My Friend and I by Lisa Jahn-Clough   The Mitten by Alvin Tresselt
    Where are Maisy's Friends? by Lucy Cousins   Friends by Helme Heine
    People by Peter Spier
    Alfie Gives a Hand by Shirley Hughes
    Will I Have a Friend by Miriam Cohen

The Creative Movement Bin: - none

The Game Bin: - none

The Snack Bin:
- one plastic zipper-locking bag for each child
- a can of mandarin oranges
- kiwi fruit
- grapes
- a can opener and knife for teacher
- plastic spoons
- bananas
- a can of fruit cocktail
- blueberries
- apples
- a large bowl
- a mixing spoon
- plastic or paper picnic bowls
- paper towels
- hand wipes

   Note: Before class, peel and slice the apples and kiwi fruit and cut them into chunks. Open the cans of mandarin oranges and fruit cocktail. Place the sliced fruit as well as the canned fruit in plastic zipper-locking bags, one bag for each child. Save the bananas, and slice them later in class.

Week 12:
- five paper plates
- peel from four lemons
- plastic sandwich bags
- a bottle of cologne or perfume
- fresh mint
- peel from three oranges
- gift wrap ribbon
- whole cloves
- dried pineapple pieces
- a Bible marked at John 12

Timesaver Option: the Before I Dream Bedtime Bible Storybook and/or the CD Before I Dream: Lord I Love You, a CD player

The Art Bin:
- paper
- preschool washable liquid paint
- paint brushes
- smocks
- newspaper or a plastic tablecloth
- packets of unsweetened powdered drink mix in colors that match the paints (for example, yellow drink mix for yellow paint, etc.)

The Science-Math Bin:
- cinnamon in a small zipper-locking bag
- a bottle of vanilla
- a jar of peanut butter
- cheese in a zipper-locking bag
- hand wipes
- bananas
- a box or bag to hide all these in

The Look and Listen Bin:
- books and/or CDs/DVDs about worship, and celebration
- CD/DVD player, if necessary
- Suggestions:
    Give Thanks to the Lord or Let's Make a Joyful Noise by Karma Wilson
    Clap Hands by Helen Oxenbury
    My Learn to Pray Bible by Karyn Henley
    Before I Dream Bedtime Bible Storybook by Karyn Henley
    Before I Dream: Lord I Love You CD by Karyn Henley
    PlaySongs: Grow, Grow, Grow CD/DVD by Karyn Henley
    PlaySongs: Tiny Treausres CD/DVD by Karyn Henley
    PlaySongs: I Feel Like a Giggle CD/DVD by Karyn Henley

The Creative Movement Bin:
- rhythm instruments (Note: You can make shakers by putting uncooked rice or dry beans or paper clips into paper lunch sacks and stapling the sacks closed.)
- streamers
- Suggestions:
    PlaySongs: Noah's Zoo by Karyn Henley
    PlaySongs: Five Little Ladybugs by Karyn Henley
    PlaySongs: I Feel Like a Giggle by Karyn Henley

The Game Bin:
- nature pictures cut out of magazines or coloring books
- a praise CD
- CD player

The Snack Bin:
- three different kinds of cheese (cheddar, a smoky-smelling cheese like Provolone, and Swiss or Parmesan cheese)
- a knife for teacher
- apple slices
- juice
- paper plates and cups
- paper towels
- hand wipes

Week 13:
- a long piece of butcher paper
- crayons and/or markers
- tape or temporary plastic adhesive (like Plasti-Tak or Tak 'n Stik)
- a Bible marked at Acts 1
- the Jesus figure and cloud figure copied and cut out from page 76

Timesaver Option: the Before I Dream Bedtime Bible Storybook

The Art Bin:
- cardboard or posterboard strips 2-inches x 8-inches
- two 6-inch strings for each child
- one 8-inch string for each child
- one 18-inch string for each child
- one Jesus figure and two cloud figures for each child copied and cut out from page 76
- cotton   - glue   - tape

The Science-Math Bin:
- cans of shaving cream
- large pieces of light blue construction paper
- liquid preschool washable watercolor paints
- paper towels
- one copy of the "Clouds" page (page 77)
- hand wipes

The Look and Listen Bin:
- books and/or CDs/DVDs about clouds and Jesus and praise
- CD/DVD player, if necessary
- Suggestions:
    The Cloud Book by Tomie dePaola
    Little Cloud by Eric Carle
    Clap Hands by Helen Oxenbury
    Give Thanks to the Lord or Let's Make a Joyful Noise by Karma Wilson
    Before I Dream Bedtime Bible Storybook by Karyn Henley
    PlaySongs: Grow, Grow, Grow CD/DVD by Karyn Henley
    PlaySongs: Tiny Treausres CD/DVD by Karyn Henley
    PlaySongs: I Feel Like a Giggle CD/DVD by Karyn Henley

The Creative Movement Bin:
- polyester fiberfill (stuffing used for pillows)
- optional: PlaySongs: Five Little Ladybugs CD/DVD by Karyn Henley, CD/DVD player

The Game Bin: - a white or blue bedsheet

The Snack Bin:
- graham crackers
- non-dairy whipped topping
- plastic picnic spoons
- juice
- paper plates and cups
- paper towels
- hand wipes